EXIT PURSUED BY A BADGER

Nick Asbury was born in Lancashire and brought up in Herefordshire, England. He went to Dartington College of Arts and studied Theatre before moving to London to work as an actor. He was lead guitarist in Arnold (1990–95) and Mookie (1999–2001) and he still works occasionally as a session pianist and guitarist for various bands and producers. He has written three plays: Trap (1992), Stuck (1994) and Cloche (1994). He now lives in Stratford-upon-Avon.

NICK ASBURY

Exit Pursued by a Badger

An Actor's Journey through History with Shakespeare

Foreword by Michael Boyd
Artistic Director, Royal Shakespeare Company

OBERON BOOKS

LONDON

First published in 2009 by Oberon Books Ltd

521 Caledonian Road, London N7 9RH

Tel 020 7607 3637   Fax 020 7607 3629

e-mail: info@oberonbooks.com

www.oberonbooks.com

A catalogue record for this book is available from the British Library.

Cover photograph by Roger Watkins.

Photographs in text by Ellie Kurttz (pp 162–74), Robert Day (p 161), Lucy Barriball (p 162), Stewart Hemley (p 175), Roger Watkins (p 176) and Keith Bartlett (p 176).

ISBN: 978-1-84002-892-8

Printed in Great Britain by CPI Antony Rowe, Chippenham.

Contents

The Histories Cast

Actor	Richard II	Henry IV Part I	Henry IV Part II
NICHOLAS ASBURY	Lord Bushy		Pistol
HANNAH BARRIE	Queen Isabel		Freda
KEITH BARTLETT	Henry Percy	Henry Percy	Henry Percy
MAUREEN BEATTIE	Duchess of York	Mistress Quickly	Mistress Quickly
ANTONY BUNSEE		Archbishop of York	Archbishop of York
ROB CARROLL	Lord Ross	Chamberlain	Fang / Wart
RICHARD CORDERY	Edmund of Langley		Lord Chief Justice
MATT COSTAIN		Gadshill	Davy / Snare
JULIUS D'SILVA		Bardolph	Bardolph
KEITH DUNPHY		Mortimer	Lord Mowbray
WELA FRASIER		Peto	Peto
GEOFFREY FRESHWATER		Carrier / Vintner	Robert Shallow
PAUL HAMILTON		Earl of Douglas	Gower / Travers / Moul
ALEXIA HEALY		Doll Tearsheet	Doll Tearsheet
KIERAN HILL		Poins	Poins
TOM HODGKINS		Earl of Westmoreland	Earl of Westmoreland
CHUK IWUJI	Duke of Gloucester		Coleville
JOHN MACKAY	Thomas Mowbray	Thomas Percy	
FORBES MASSON	Bagot / Lord Marshall		Rumour
CHRIS McGILL		John of Lancaster / Francis	John of Lancaster
PATRICE NAIAMBANA			Earl of Warwick
LUKE NEAL	Lord Willoughby / Vernon	Vernon	Servant to Lord Chief Justice / Bullcalf
SANDY NEILSON	Bishop of Carlisle		Silence
ANN OGBOMO	Lady	Lady Percy (Kate)	Lady Percy
MILES RICHARDSON		Sir Walter Blunt	Lord Bardolph
LEX SHRAPNEL	Harry Percy	Harry Percy (Hotspur)	
ANTHONY SHUSTER	Green	Soldier	Clarence / Shadow
JONATHAN SLINGER	Richard II		Ghost of Richard II
KATY STEPHENS	Duchess of Gloucester		Francis Feeble
GEOFFREY STREATFEILD		Prince Hal	Prince Hal
JAMES TUCKER	Duke of Aumerle		Lord Hastings
DAVID WARNER		Sir John Falstaff	Sir John Falstaff
ROGER WATKINS	John of Gaunt	Owen Glendower / Carrier	
CLIVE WOOD	Henry Bolingbroke	Henry IV	Henry IV

Henry V	Henry VI Part I	Henry VI Part II	Henry VI Part III	Richard III
Pistol	Somerset	Somerset	Somerset	2nd Murderer
Alice	Fiend	Margery Jourdain	Attendant	Lady Anne
	Talbot	Ghost of Talbot	Father who killed his son	Stanley
Mistress Quickly		Eleanor, Duchess of Gloucester		Duchess of York
Constable	Keeper	Keeper	Keeper	Brackenbury
MacMorris / Sir Thomas Grey				
	Humphrey	Humphrey	Louis XI	Buckingham
Duke of Burgundy	Burgundy	Humphrey Stafford	Montague	Ratcliffe
Bardolph	Sir William Lucy	Peter	Rutland's Tutor	Catesby
Nym	Young Clifford	Young Clifford	Lord Clifford	1st Murderer/Lovell
Peto/Boy	Gunner's Boy	Keeper's Assistant	Prince Edward	Lord Mayor's Attendant
Archbishop of Canterbury	Winchester	Cardinal Beaufort		Scrivener
Captain Gower	Alexander Eden	Alexander Eden	Oxford	Oxford
Katherine	Fiend	Simpcox's Wife	Lady Bona	Mistress Shore
Duke of Orleans	Mayor's Officer	Horner	Westmoreland	Lord Mayor
Earl of Westmoreland	Bedford	Duke of Buckingham	Hastings	Hastings
Montjoy	Henry VI	Henry VI	Henry VI	Ghost of Henry VI
Dauphin	Dauphin	Jack Cade	Sir John Montgomery	Tyrell
Chorus	Alençon	Edward	Edward	Edward IV
Duke of Bedford	Sir William Stafford	Sir William Stafford	Northumberland	Grey
Earl of Warwick	Earl of Warwick	Earl of Warwick	Earl of Warwick	Ghost of Warwick
Gloucester				
King of France				
	Fiend	Margaret's Attendant	Elizabeth	Elizabeth
Duke of Exeter	Duke of Exeter	Lord Clifford	Duke of Exeter	Bishop of Ely
Michael Williams	John Talbot	Ghost of John Talbot	Son who killed his father	Richmond
Bates / Cambridge		Soldier	Soldier	
Captain Fluellen	Bastard of Orleans	Richard	Richard	Richard III
Queen Isabel of France	Joan of Arc	Queen Margaret	Queen Margaret	Queen Margaret
Henry V	Suffolk	Suffolk	Rivers	Rivers
Scroop / Prisoner	Reignier	George	George	George (Clarence)
Bishop of Ely	Edmund Mortimer	Earl of Salisbury	Duke of Norfolk	Archbishop of York
	Richard Plantagenet	Richard Plantagenet	Richard Plantagenet	Ghost of York

Family Tree of Edward III

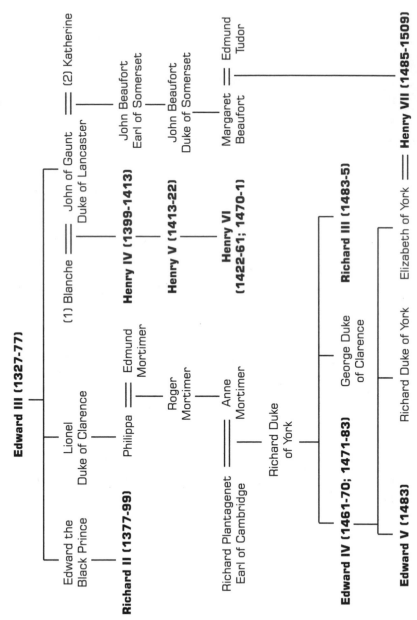

Foreword by Michael Boyd

HAUNTED but still haughty, Nick Asbury enters upstage centre as the Earl of Somerset to announce the loss of France to an internecine English court. Later his pedantic, but compassionate Murderer is at a loss with a machete and a victim, and later still his Pistol is completely smashed to pieces by the end of *Henry V* but reassembles himself like Tom after the definitive Jerry victory and teeters back to England determined to survive. These are three of my random favourite moments of Nick Asbury's performances in *The Histories Cycle*.

This Blog from the belly of *The Histories* beast gives a great insight into how he got there, how we all recovered from our losses, and survived to create something of real worth.

Other members of the company and production team would have produced very different blogs, but I'm sure all are grateful that Nick had the stamina and made the time to share his experience of mounting the project.

I don't know why Nick started. Perhaps it was therapy, a cry for help, a message in a bottle from the desert island of our rehearsal room. Or maybe Clea and Nada from Press suggested it. Whatever the motivation, it's a great read, thanks to Nick's self-sacrificial humour, and engaging storytelling. Not to mention the odd insight into acting.

Thank you Nick for being such a generous, spirited host to our extended audience. Whatever the time of day or night, undeterred by fatigue, injury or the lamentable state of your personal hygiene, you were always there to open the door and show us around your *Histories*.

Acknowledgements

THERE are so many people I could thank for their help in this book that it would take another book to list them all, but here are a few whose direct involvement helped so much. Thank you.

Everyone in the Who's Who section in this book (pp 181–4) deserves my fullest thanks and praise, but all at The Royal Shakespeare Company who work tirelessly to bring Shakespeare to the stage should be thanked. Clea Boorman at the RSC was the main mover and shaker behind setting up the original idea of the Blog and I'm eternally grateful to her for putting up with all my missives and publishing them originally on the RSC website. Suzanne Worthington at the RSC for checking the introduction; Nada Zakula in the Press Office for fielding all my questions; Kevin Wright for giving me some names and for sitting through photograph sessions trying to choose which ones of the hundreds that exist. Geoffrey Lumb, for reading through the text and pointing out a couple of reminders. Ellie Kurttz and the RSC for the use of her wonderful photographs, and the photographers Robert Day, Lucy Barriball and Stewart Hemley. My fellow actors Roger Watkins for his great photographs, and Keith Bartlett for the table tennis shot.

Thanks to all at Oberon Books, especially Stephen Watson, who has worked tirelessly to turn this into something respectable, and James Hogan who believed in it from the start.

Thanks to the people who responded to the Blog when it was on the RSC website and especially to those whose responses I have included in the book. As is stated often enough, they, the audience, were as much a part of the shows as any of us.

The Histories Ensemble. We did it. I miss you all. And thank you for letting me write about you.

To Michael Boyd who not only wrote a Foreword to this book but gave me a job in the first place and changed my life as a consequence. He created this whole thing. His vision and leadership are extraordinary.

Hannah, for her belief and courage.

Finally, whilst this book is dedicated to my Father, to my Mother go all the thanks in the world. She it is who has had to put up with a husband and three sons who have never stopped dreaming. She enabled us all and still does.

In memory of

Bruce Hamilton (1926–2007)

Duke Mbusi (1950–2006)

Ian Richardson (1934–2007)

Three fathers which the Histories Company lost.

Terry Bennett, Technical Manager at The Courtyard (2008)

In celebration of

Rua Lilias Masson Robertson. Conceived, born and had her first birthday during the whole project. That's what I call making history. She even walked onto the stage at The Roundhouse and said a few words...

To my Father,
Who let me dream and play.

Introduction

THE idea was nuts. Absolutely nuts.

To stage *eight* of Shakespeare's History Plays from *Richard II*, via *Henry IV Parts I & II, Henry V, Henry VI Parts I, II & III* to *Richard III*. And if that just looks like a maths equation and a jumble of names then you're not far off what I felt. To use the same company of actors, the same director, the same designers, creative team, stage crew, everything and everybody, throughout. An ensemble.

For *two and a half years*.

From February 2006 to June 2008, this crazy idea was to be achieved by the Royal Shakespeare Company, one of the biggest theatre companies in the world. Although they, and others, had staged massive 'History' projects before, never had all these plays been done together in their entirety. Not since Shakespeare's own troupe of actors, 400 years ago, had they been done pretty much uncut by one group of theatremakers. Michael Boyd, the Artistic Director of the RSC, from whose fevered brain this idea sprang, was to be the Director for the whole thing.

And I had been cast in it.

For the last year and a half of that extraordinary time, as one of the actors in this insane project, I kept a Blog on the Royal Shakespeare Company website, detailing some of the ups and downs of life in a world of swords, words, blood, magic and sheer hard work. This is the book of that Blog.

IT all began six years before, in the Spring of the year 2000, when I met Michael Boyd for the first time in one of the airless rooms that used to be the Royal Shakespeare Company offices in the Barbican

Centre in London. I was understudying Konstantin in the then Artistic Director Adrian Noble's RSC production of *The Seagull* at the Barbican, and I had had a phone call the day before saying that Michael wanted to see me for the part of the Duke of Somerset in his forthcoming RSC production of *Henry VI Parts I, II & III*. That evening, before, during and after the show, I desperately started reading these frankly mystifying plays. All these blokes with the names of English Counties shouting at each other.

By the time I met him the next day I'd got to midway through *Part II* and was pretty much none the wiser as to what was going on. Michael sympathised and began to explain what he wanted to do: to tell the story plainly and simply using the dynamics of an ensemble of actors all portraying events through physical imagery and committed playing. We read a scene from *Part I* – the Temple Garden scene – where all the protagonists, the Duke of Somerset included, argue and then pick red or white roses to determine who is on whose side, which sets off a chain of events leading to the main theme of these three History Plays: the Wars of the Roses.

I got the part. And from that moment my life changed.

We rehearsed all three plays in London and even during that time it was pretty clear that something special was going on. We transformed The Swan Theatre in Stratford-upon-Avon, the beautiful wooden Elizabethanesque galleried theatre at the back of the main Royal Shakespeare Theatre building, into the 'round', where the audience circle the stage. We used every single facet of the theatre: we entered from above the stage, below it, through the audience, around them. Through the massive metal double doors which formed the centrepiece of a set which was in effect the whole theatre. A cathedral of sounds, smells, visual heroics and breathtaking action. All clearly telling the story I had found so difficult to unravel when reading, but which, through Michael's genius at staging, had become a riveting, clear, rollicking action drama.

Whilst performing them we rehearsed *Richard III*, Shakespeare's sequel to his *Henry VI* plays. We opened that in Stratford, and from there took all four plays to America and the Young Vic Theatre in

London. It broke through a few barriers and won Michael an Olivier Award for Best Director and a South Bank Show Award for Best Theatre Production. It was a revelation to me in theatre making, storytelling, design and concept. And also in the understanding, camaraderie and exceptional hard work of playing in a troupe of actors.

It was a wonderful time and launched me into a completely different set of parts when the whole thing finished in the summer of 2001. Suddenly, finally, I started getting offered bigger and better parts. I had a career. Hurrah. In so many ways – artistically, socially, professionally – this job had changed my life.

Then, in the summer of 2005, I got a phone call from my agent saying would I go in and have a chat with Michael who, by this time, had been made Artistic Director of the RSC. Michael sat me down and casually explained that he wanted to stage it again. 'Are you alright?' was my only reply. But this time he wanted to double it and do the four prequels Shakespeare had written to the three *Henry VIs* and *Richard III*, namely: *Richard II*, *Henry IV Parts I & II* and *Henry V*.

Just like that.

A brief pause for me to take this in. Nuts. Absolutely nuts. He asked would I do it? I took about, ooh, a second to answer – and with that the next three years of my life were taken care of. Which, for an actor, is a barely imaginable amount of time and job security.

I still couldn't imagine, however, how on earth we were going to do it. The sheer physical and mental demands of learning and performing just four of these History Plays had been exhausting enough. Now to do another four on top of that seemed almost impossible. Like having scaled one mountain only to be told that you have to do it again and then conquer another peak as well.

I remembered a moment when we had first staged these monumental plays back in 2000. Every Saturday we would perform all three plays in one day. A 'Trilogy' day, starting with *Henry VI Part I* at 10.30 in the morning, *Part II* at 3.00 in the afternoon and then *Part III* at 7.30 in the evening. The first time we did one of these days I was dumbstruck. I couldn't believe we were doing it. Us and the audience, together in a theatre, for over twelve hours. Could we pull it off? Surely we were mad to think so. I remember ten minutes into the show being on a ladder 50 feet up in the roof of the Swan Theatre, ready to be lowered in and do a scene which was suspended a good twenty feet off the ground, and then be blown off that ladder by an actor swinging across the length of the theatre on a rope and hang, my entire head covered in blood, whilst a battle raged below me. Then be brought back up into the gods, get off the ladder (no mean feat when your eyes are sealed with fake blood) and go and do the next twelve hours of the shows.

Clutching desperately onto that ladder before the scene, gripped with trouser-changing fear – it's high up there, and you're trying not to look down or else the audience might get more than they bargained for – I just could not imagine how we were going to do it. I mean, there was just so much that could go wrong. So many lines, cues, entrances, exits, moves, rope climbs, swordfights, deaths and misdemeanours that could end up going haywire, it was inevitable. Daunting. But I resolved just to take it scene by scene. Catch the wave, just go for it and see where you are by 11 o'clock that evening. Hopefully in the pub with a well-deserved pint and a feeling of accomplishment I have never had before. The cue came to go, the green light went on, I gave the ladder operator a nod and down I went into that cauldron. That pint was the best I ever tasted.

Now to do it all again and double it. Good God. And what's more, we were going to do it in a theatre twice the size of The Swan that hadn't even been built yet.

In 2004, a year after Michael had taken over as Artistic Director, the RSC announced they were going to completely redevelop the main Royal Shakespeare Memorial Theatre at their base in Stratford-upon-Avon. In order to continue performing whilst the three-year building project ran, they would transform The Other Place (the smallest of the RSC's three theatres in Stratford – The Swan being the other) into a foyer and in the car park outside would build a 1000-seat temporary construction, called The Courtyard Theatre, as the template of what the main Theatre could become. To celebrate this they were going to stage a Complete Works Festival from April 23 (Shakespeare's birthday) 2006 to April 2007, whereby every play, every sonnet, every word written by the great man would be performed over the course of a year in the three theatres that would, for a while, overlap.

The Courtyard Theatre became, as the press called it, 'at once, one of the most loved theatres in Britain', and it was our job, in what was rapidly becoming called 'The Histories Ensemble', to open it. Built around the idea of the Elizabethan Globe Theatre, but massively bigger in scale, the audience are positioned around a huge 'thrust' stage in a horseshoe shape, so they are so much closer to the action. There are the stalls, then two more galleries of seats which tower over the stage and the audience below, making a bear-pit of noise and excitement. The actors can enter from the towering wall at the back of the stage, or through the audience on massive walkways or simply using the aisles that the audience use to get to their seats. You can come from above, the side, on a different level, and from underneath. It is three-dimensional, vast, but incredibly intimate too. And as they built this theatre so we began to build our plays.

All our rehearsing would be done in London and the shows would be staged in Stratford. For the first year we would stage *Henry VI Parts I, II & III* and *Richard III*. For the second we would do the prequels *Richard II, Henry IV Parts I & II* and *Henry V*. In the third we would bring all eight together as an 'Octology' culminating in "The Glorious Moment' where we would play them all in four days in (historically) chronological order in Stratford. Then play them all for a few months in London at The Roundhouse.

Simple, really.

We were starting in the middle of the 'Octology', but at least Michael and six of us from the previous incarnation in 2000/1 had done it before, so it seemed sensible to start such a massive project from a position of at least knowing *something* about what we were doing. A template had been established so we could use that as a platform, or base camp, from which to launch our assault. So, first up, we were starting with the three *Henry VIs*, rehearsing these in London for eighteen weeks – six weeks a play – and then sticking them on in Stratford during the summer. Then back to London to rehearse *Richard III* and stage that and the other three in Stratford. This was the first year. Same template for the other plays the next year. As easy as that.

If you had to read through that last paragraph again in order to make any sense of it, you begin to get some idea of what we were all going through that first morning.

Any first day of rehearsals is daunting enough. You're meeting loads of new people you're going to be spending lots of time with in the future. Like the first day of school. You're going to be judged. All the insecurities, tensions, battles, openness, inspiration, status games, love and joy of meeting new people are spread before you like a feast. But here, we were facing two and a half years of working, playing and being together. That's longer than university or drama school, if you take out all their holidays. Some of us knew each other, of course. Some had been at the RSC for the last year performing in the previous ensemble. Others, like me, had been in the original *Henry VIs*, so could find a friendly face. For others it was their first time with the company. All of us vaguely ashen-faced and perplexed, but excited and ready to go. What was going to happen?

We kept the Announcements column in the newspapers quite busy for the next two and a half years. We had three fathers die, one marriage, an engagement and a baby born during the time we were together. But all of that was ahead of us. For now, Michael sat us down and slowly all the actors, designers, voice coaches, stage management, press officers, wardrobe technicians – all the intricate bundle of very talented people, the ensemble, that work to put on any RSC show, let alone the biggest production they've ever staged in their history – introduced themselves.

Suddenly we were into it. Mercifully, there wasn't a 'read-through' – the normal tortuous ritual for actors and production crew alike as they sit around listening to us mangle our way through little-known or semi-digested text. We'd have been there for days if that had happened. Tom Piper, Chief Associate Designer at the RSC, explained to us with a little model how the set and theatre might look. Taking the 'thrust' stage as his lead, the back wall of the stage was to be a huge semi-circle of rusting metal 40 feet high. High up in this wall, level with the second gallery of the theatre, the four musicians, led by Jimmy Jones and his assortment of drums, marimbas, vibraphones, sheets of metal, blocks of wood, bells and whistles, would commentate on and punctuate the action happening down below or sometimes way up above.

In the middle of the concave semi-circle of metal which made up the back wall would be a placed a huge monolithic circular metal tower stretching from the stage to the lighting grid up above, with different balconies used as performance areas; at ground level it consisted of a massive set of double doors which could be used as anything from an entrance or exit, to a battlement, a room in a palace or house, a place from which to hang someone, or an entrance to heaven or hell.

The rest of the stage, thrusting into the audience as they horseshoe around it, would be covered in metal but entirely free of anything save a series of trapdoors, which again could be used to signify anything from a grave to a hiding place, a battle trench or, indeed, a brothel.

The rest of the theatre, including all the aisles and audience areas on every level would again be as much a part of the 'set' as anything on stage. Ropes and ladders would be used at times, not only to get from one part of the theatre to another but to enter and exit, be trees, strangle someone, attack, fight. How we would do all that was up to us...

Michael gave us a brief overview of how he hoped things would work. He told us that in the second year we would all get a play off. Which was nice. To facilitate this, five or six more actors would be brought in at the start of the second year. But importantly, he told us we were there not only to rehearse, but to learn, to grow, to experiment. To create a world where all the dynamics of theatre and our craft could sing out and excel, and thus this great story spanning 100 years of English history could be told with a vigour, passion and trust that our audience could share in and be thrilled by. Easier said than done. Then, just like that, it was, take a deep breath, Act One, Scene One, Part One.

The first few weeks of any theatrical company is an important time, but here we had the opportunity to start really getting to know each other and work out how we were going to survive in each other's company over the next two years.

We were given lectures as a company on English medieval history, Shakespeare and Catholicism, and the History Plays themselves, by visiting professors and experts. On verse speaking. We even had a tutorial on Rhetoric by the world public speaking champion Benedict Brandreth. Later on, during *Richard III*, Shami Chakrabati, the head of the human rights activist group Liberty, spoke to us about the nature of tyranny. Each one of the lectures was accompanied by an excited visit to the pub afterwards and the increasingly flowing mix of chatter, debate and interest that brings.

Michael even brought in an African drumming band for us all to dance to, so we could start freeing up and using our bodies in new and interesting ways. We all had to dance individually at one point, within the circle of the rest of us clapping and cheering, and whilst it was achingly fearsome and embarrassing for me – I dance like a fly that's flown into a toaster – the happy smiles and loud whistles that accompanied everybody, Michael and all the creative team included, as they span and writhed to the beat for a few bars, signified that we were getting somewhere.

We began to play. After one particularly tricky morning trying to find our way through the stormy Parliament scene in Act 3 of *Part I*, we were tired and not a little down. During lunch, however, a few of us found an old basketball and began just to throw it to each other; quickly it became a game which more and more people joined as they drifted back from lunch. By the end there we all were delighting in just throwing and catching a ball with each other, laughing, joking and smiling, like an advert for a Swedish campsite. Michael sat, with a certain paternal grace, and eventually after a long while suggested we might get back to work. That afternoon we nailed that Parliament scene.

By the time we had our first 'run-through' of *Henry VI Part I*, we were already gelling. It had been a long four weeks for everyone, facing up to such a huge task, and to look at what we'd got in our first stumblings together was a big moment. This was our first sketch on a large canvas and it was nerve-wracking and thrilling to play it out in front of each other. We managed to get through it, and this was the first time where I, and I know others, began to think that this could work. Not only that, but this could be brilliant. Something was happening here and it was very, very exciting.

As often happens with these big projects, we spent seven weeks on *Part I* and a further seven on *Part II*, which of course meant we only had four weeks to rehearse *Part III*. But by that time we were flying. I felt as though I had known these people forever and already I was making lifelong friends. We had started to develop a language. A way of working whereby we formed an almost code-like form of communication. So that, although we were pressed for time on *Part III*, all the legwork had been done. We could attack the scenes with gusto, knowing how we could play around with them, serve them properly and above tell the story in as exciting and illuminating a way as possible.

It wasn't all plain sailing of course. The Cade scenes in *Part II*, where Jack Cade, played by John Mackay, stages a rebellion against King Henry, were especially difficult. We'd had the idea of Cade coming in on a trapeze and launching his manifesto, and character, from there. That's all very good in theory, but try rehearsing that in a room that's not built for such things. A large sort of frame was built for John to swing about on, but whilst every day he was working out and practising trapeze work on his own, by the time he came into a smaller room with all of us bellowing and exhorting, he had to completely change everything and just ended up nutting himself on the ceiling. We just had to imagine how it was going to pan out most of the time, and it was not until we got into the theatre that we really began to find out what should happen. Nerve-wracking for all of us, not least for John, but we got through it.

John had never been near a trapeze in his life before, let alone perform on one, but once the decision was made he was training every day. Eventually, a year and a half later whilst rehearsing *Henry V*, he was so good on the trapeze that Michael stuck him on it as the Dauphin for pretty much the entire show and got all the other 'French' to do the same. Thus, the shows developed a language, and symmetry, of their own.

We had blobs, slideys, and Barnets. A Jimmy 'douf' rather than a Jimmy 'bong'. An Asbury ring, and even a King Blob.

The 'blob' became a generic term for any group piece of abstract movement used by the company of actors to tell a story. The mother of these 'blobs' was a section in *Henry VI Part I*, created in order to dramatise the impossible and overwhelming odds faced by the English warriors, Lord Talbot and his son, at a battle where they meet their deaths in France. We developed a slow motion, abstract piece where the entire company faced the two Talbots and gradually enveloped them in a wave of martial bodies, eventually slaying and hoisting them aloft, leaving the young Talbot (played by Lex Shrapnel) suspended high above the stage in a sling, lifeless and bloodied. Cue much ribald laughing and joshing, as we spent about three days working solidly with Liz Rankin our Movement Director, and Terry King our Fight Director, on what would actually work and how the story could most dramatically and effectively be told.

For actors, these are the weirdest moments: you're flailing your arms about in an odd fashion, feeling very stupid (as is everyone else), but you are working together and creating things. The trouble is, as a group, we have no idea what it looks like from the outside – so you have to take it on trust that the Creatives, who are all watching, have some idea about what they're doing and don't leave you looking like a loon. It means a hell of a lot of hanging about as others discuss what could be done better to make it work. Then it's back to flinging your arms and legs about, slowly, in what you hope is an artfully pleasing way, whilst a fellow cast member's face is two inches from your own and you can tell what the so-and-so had for breakfast that morning. Kind of brings you closer together.

The 'King Blob' was a similar piece of movement to symbolise the climactic fight at the end of *Henry IV Part I*: everyone was dressed as the King to confuse the enemy. We had a moment at the start of *Richard II* where the whole cast, dressed for this play in Elizabethan finery, did a slow motion Tudor Pavanne dance in unison to introduce the audience to the world of the show. This became the Pavanne Blob. Simple.

Slideys. Ah, slideys. Terry King, our Fight Director, as well as being a general *über*-person, has taught 'Fighting' in drama schools and been a Fight Director over the last twenty years or so, and most people who have had to fight on an English stage over that period will have come across him at one time or another. He has a weird and wonderful vocabulary of bangs and crashes, hits and strokes. One of them being the 'slidey', where one fighter with a broadsword hangs their sword out to the left or right at an angle from shoulder height and the other attacking fighter gives it an almighty wallop. It looks very spectacular and is completely safe to all concerned.

As well as all the usual thrusts, parries, head shots and cuts, the vocabulary seeps into you as you become able to create a fight very quickly, based around the story. And, boy, did we have to create them quickly. I worked it out that in *Henry VI Parts I, II & III* there were thirty-three individual broadsword fights. Many were extraordinary stand-alone set-pieces, and some took place within the context of bigger fights. The Battle of Barnet, the huge climactic fight towards the end of *Henry VI Part III* where the Yorkists finally beat the Lancastrians and the Earl of Warwick is slain, involved fifteen of us fighting on the stage with broadswords at the same time, with Clive Wood as the Ghost of the Duke of York walking through the middle of it all. Not only did this involve intense choreography, but Clive had to take it on trust that we weren't going to brain him.

The broadswords we used are long bits of aircraft steel shaped into a sword and are solid throughout so they give a satisfying metallic ring as they are hit, as well as being capable of taking your head off. I, as Fight Captain on all the seven shows I was in, would remind everyone that if that ring begins to dull, then the metal was probably beginning to fracture under the hilt and could break when used to fight. I was particularly keen to stress what became known as the 'Asbury ring' because in the 2000 staging of the *Henry VIs*, one actor had hit the metal doors with his sword during a performance and the weakened metal, having gone unspotted, broke in two. It flew from the hilt, sliced open the actor's forehead and went pinging across the stage. He did his entire death speech with blood pouring down his face, and the audience must have sat there thinking how clever the special effects were.

Fights, in general, are dangerous – Barnet especially so, and Terry worked out each actor's strokes and movements minutely before we put it all together. This had then to be practised every day to get it right and once achieved, be run through (an unfortunate choice of words on this occasion) before every show. We had a fight 'call' before every show on every day of those two and a half years. As Fight Captain, it was my job to keep an eye on them all and let my fellow actors know if anything was beginning to creep in that was dangerous or unsafe. And also to teach the understudies the fight, which meant I had to learn the moves for every fight, which frankly is nigh-on impossible – but I did know when things were wrong. When done right they are as thrilling a moment as any in theatre, but they are very perilous.

Even though the swords are blunt, they could still kill given the force with which they are wielded. Doing a fight call once before a show, two of the guys had one of the very, very few little spats that we ever had over the two years. We were all knackered, and over that amount of time there's bound to be the odd flashpoint. The only problem was, they were standing there shouting at each other with swords in their hands, which raised the stakes somewhat, in my view. 'Er, lads, lads! Er, put the swords down! Put the... Whoah!!' A few of us calmed the situation and within minutes all had made up and were laughing about it. But the RSC, in their wisdom, put TV screens of the stage out in the foyer and our little contretemps was seen by many of the audience, milling about before the show. Chris McGill's parents were in that day, both of whom had seen the show before, and remarked to Chris how they had never seen that particular fight. Get out of that one, matey...

Jimmy Jones, of course, had seen them all before. He is the musical genius who created the percussive music throughout the shows. He was in rehearsals with us all the time, right from the beginning of the creative process, and at one end of the main rehearsal room in Clapham he had set up a vast array of percussive instruments and sheets of metal to play with. And as we began to form each scene, so Jimmy would be just as much a part of it as any of the actors, punctuating moments with a vocabulary of 'tings', shakers, bangs and wallops. And of course as we carried on, so our vernacular began to include whether we could have a 'douf' rather than a 'bang' or the like – subtle differences which meant the story could be told better.

Gradually, scene by scene, we knitted it all together. Rehearsals generally started with a warm-up in the morning and then straight into work on whatever scene we were on. In other parts of the building, Alison Bomber, the RSC's Senior Voice and Text Coach, would work with actors not only on how they sounded, but on the words. The WORDS. Shakespeare is difficult, make no mistake, and it is our job as actors to communicate. If we don't understand what we're going on about, then how are the audience going to? All of us had many a breakthrough session with Alison, going through speeches, plotting our way. And working on our voice, too. You can't sit there bellowing for two and half years to a thousand-strong audience and not have proper support for your voice and how you use it. What's the point, if you can't be heard?

Elsewhere Terry would be working on a fight, or Liz would be going through a piece of movement. Matt Costain, who was in the cast but is also a genius on rope and all things circus, was our Director of Ropework, and would lead actors who had never gone near a rope before in training sessions, so that in the end they all looked like Tarzan on the things.

Our Associate Director on the project, Richard Twyman, would take other rehearsals, going over scenes we had already done, trying to perfect them. Our Assistant Director, Donnacadh O'Briain, would take understudy rehearsals sometimes stretching long into the evening, so any working day could last from ten in the morning to nine or ten at night. In this ensemble, everybody understudied everybody else, so there wasn't the old hierarchy of 'lead' actors swanning about whilst others worked on past their bedtime. Understandably, if you had a big role in one play then you would have a tiny understudy part, but if your role was smaller in another play then you were given a correspondingly bigger part to cover. Not all the parts fitted uniformly into this mould which meant that some people inevitably ended up learning more than others. But, in the end, it bred a much more 'ensemble' feel. We were, bar the odd line or two here and there, in it together.

And what an amount of lines we had to learn. Not only did we have to learn our own parts for seven plays, combining all our understudy parts we had to learn fourteen plays. And it's not just the words.

The whole journey around the theatre for each character; the fights, rope work, blood spills, emotions, everything involved in portraying somebody on that stage had to be chewed and digested ready for performance.

Ready or not, we did our final run-throughs on our last Friday and Saturday in London and we had the weekend to move to Stratford-upon-Avon. Even though we were behind on *Part III*, we were straining at the leash. It was time, after eighteen weeks, to start putting it all in front of people. Actors, directors, designers all need that final piece of the jigsaw, the audience, to begin to have a real sense of how the show is going to perform. What works, what doesn't. What can be cut, what needs to be added. Michael uses this period over the first week or two – the previews – to its full capacity. So you find yourself performing in the evening and all the adrenalin that involves, then you're back like a boomerang the next morning working on stuff again. And when you've three plays to put on, that's a long time to be doing that. It's relentless, very hard work and extraordinarily tiring; but it pays off.

That weekend was the most excited I'd ever felt about doing a show. We had, I thought, something just a little bit special here and it was now our time to introduce it to the Bard, at his final resting place in Stratford-upon-Avon and see what he thought, lying there in his grave not 400 yards from where we going to perform.

· ·

STRATFORD-UPON-AVON is a wonderful, strange, old place. The ancient Warwickshire town is one of the most perfect expressions of Old England in the country, with its centre of beautiful higgledy-piggledy buildings lining market streets filled with restaurants and shops catering for the mass of visitors which descend every year. The River Avon potters slowly through the town past Holy Trinity Church where Shakespeare was christened, married and buried. Willows weep into its waters, and towering over it the great theatres stand guard, built in honour of arguably the greatest writer of all time.

Ranged around these theatres are a mish-mash of Victorian, Georgian and Tudor buildings which the Royal Shakespeare Company fill with offices, wardrobe departments, an armoury and actors' accommodation. Any actor coming up to this old town from London, reversing the path Shakespeare made in his search for glory, but no less wondrous, is thrown headlong into a whirl of stages and history, life and community. One of the beauties, and for some actors, complete terror, about Stratford is that it's not London. It's a small place and the world of the theatres is even smaller, so it tends to focus your mind not only on The Plays but on the whole 'living in an ensemble' feel. It can be suffocating, threatening and claustrophobic, but also safe, intriguing and wonderfully releasing. It is a place of dreams, if you let it.

Most of the actors stay in accommodation close by. Waterside, the street passing in front of the theatres and the town, has a line of beautiful terraced cottages, all white wooden doors and hanging baskets, which are used each year by actors of differing hygiene and party habits. Avonside, round the other side of the church, is a block of flats filled with achingly thin walls and actors with loud voices. Next to the old ferry on Waterside is the Ferryhouse and the Malthouse: old, old buildings which have been converted into rooms for the actors and far too close to the Dirty Duck for comfort.

This ancient pub sits in between the three theatres and has been the focal point of social life for any actor in Stratford for what seems a thousand years. The ghosts of many an old actor nestle by the fire as the shouts and screams and drinks and songs and snogs ring around the old place.

In the summer of 2006, when we arrived, it was jumping. The Complete Works Festival was in full swing: as well as two companies of RSC actors, one staging *Romeo and Juliet*, *King John*, *Much Ado About Nothing* and the other *The Tempest*, *Julius Caesar* and *Antony and Cleopatra*, there were actors and performers from all over the world putting on their own version of a particular Shakespeare play. That summer alone there were South Africans performing *Hamlet*, Americans doing *Henry IV*, Brazilians with *Two Gentleman of Verona*, Japanese staging *Titus Andronicus* and many more theatre companies from all over Britain putting on their plays. It truly was a festival and the back garden of the Dirty Duck would thrum in turn to samba drumming from the Brazilians, or South Africans singing songs of freedom. The atmosphere was electric.

When I had first arrived in Stratford in the winter of 1999, thereby realising a long-cherished dream and ambition, it could not have been more different. Morale was low and, I couldn't believe it, but actors just didn't want to be there. Now, the place was humming and it felt more like the Edinburgh Festival with so many people from all over the world performing, watching, playing and enjoying. Clive Wood and I, having worked on the previous Henries together, had got a great place in one of the cottages on Waterside and from there I was in a wonderful position to sample everything that Stratford had to offer. And I could set about my personal mission to rival the Dirty Duck in hospitality. Tough on Clive and the liver, but great for the soul.

What's more, our theatre, The Courtyard, hadn't even been finished yet. As we were shown around, there were still people hammering and knocking bits together. Some seats still had to be put into place and the curving corner pieces which connect the auditorium to the wall of the stage were yet to be fitted. So as we began technical rehearsals for *Henry VI Part I*, it was accompanied by drills and clanging from the small army of builders and technicians assembled to get the thing up on time. And our own army of actors, stage crew, lighting and sound, automation (all the flying effects), wardrobe, wigs and make-up, directors and designers were now swinging into action too.

This is always an exciting time, when, after weeks of hard work, the show begins to materialise. The Technical Rehearsal, or the 'Tech', is the labour of a show. After weeks of gestation, out it comes. Lights and sound and set are all created and delivered. All the 'flying', where actors and bits of set are lifted in and out on steel wires, is painstakingly etched out. For actors, it's nerve-wracking and breathless in equal measure. You can sit around for ever, waiting for some technical piece of wizardry to be plotted in and then suddenly you're on, shouting and whooping. Everyone's in costume. For the first time you get to see the vision of the creative team as all these wonderful pieces of clothing, hand-made and pored over with so much care by the RSC Costume Department, shimmer before you.

And what a world we were in. I think the only way to describe the look of the show is 'suggested medieval'. Big boots, leather trousers, and long sweeping cloaks for the boys, with sword belts and broadswords hanging to our side. Beautiful flowing dresses for the girls. Grey, almost modern-looking uniforms for the English army. Blue for the French army. A simple breastplate over a smock for Joan of Arc.

They looked spectacular and when put onto the huge metal set that had been built, with its massive central tower and monolithic walls, the whole theatre, let alone the stage, was breathtaking. Our very own warehouse of noises and words and dreams had been created yet again.

The show starts on a happy note with the funeral of *Henry V*. So into the main downstage trap, right in the heart of the audience as they envelop the stage in their enormous horseshoe, the coffin of Henry is lowered from high up in the lighting grid above the stage. This was done by some of the actors on a series of pulleys operated by ropes from the stage, and as it sank so we processed on stage to mourn at the 'grave'. Accompanied by the wailing of women, smoke and incense, and the dark, low rhythms of the massive drums up above, the ghost of Henry V (played by Geoffrey Streatfeild who would play Henry V the following year, thereby completing our History Cycle) came down the spiralling stairs in the metal tower and emerged through the big double doors to wander spectrally through the bickering lords he left behind at his death.

With a vomit of blood over his own coffin he slithers into his grave and lies on top of the coffin as the scene unfolds and finally, the large, heavy, metal doors of the trap are slammed over him by the new world order above. As you can imagine, that's a pretty tricky opener to get right. To get the timing right so Geoffrey knew when to get to the grave at exactly the right point in the scene; to get the coffin into place in time; to make sure Geoffrey wasn't flattened like roadkill when the doors of the trap were thrown shut above him; for the drumming to be in the right time; everything worked out and nothing left to chance.

That takes time. And that was just the first scene of the first play out of EIGHT!

It also introduced the audience to one of the main motifs that Michael used within the plays to tell and aid the story. Ghosts of characters would appear on stage at regular intervals, commenting and looking at the action, their presence reminding the audience of why events were happening, and the consequences of that ghost's death. Even though the actor playing the part would go on to other roles, those new parts might have echoes of their previous characters in the story. So, for example, Keith Dunphy and I played Clifford and Somerset respectively – both stalwarts of the Lancastrian red rose faction against the Yorkist white rose side. After we were killed, some hours later in a different play (*Richard III*), we came back as the murderers to kill one of the main Yorkist leaders, the Duke of Clarence, played by Jimmy Tucker. Which we did with a machete. Then in *Henry V*, we both, as Pistol and Nym, carried machetes to fight with in France and I, as Pistol, accosted a French prisoner, played by Jimmy, with my machete. Jimmy finds it difficult to look at a machete without blanching even now.

Gradually we worked our way through it. Through the fighting in France and the loss of Lord Talbot. The arguing over the new boy king at home and the splitting of the most powerful lords into two factions – one symbolised by white roses, the other red. And thence to *Part II* and the political intrigue and infighting, leading to a rebellion with Jack Cade at its head, and the Duke of York claiming the throne. Then the climactic *Part III* where what has now become the Wars of the Roses spills into chaos and we see the youngest son of the Duke of York, ignored by everyone because of the hump on his back and a withered leg, later to be crowned as Richard III, emerge as the chief villain and powerbroker of the story. Phew.

An average day when you are 'teching' starts at ten and finishes at ten. With lunch and tea off in between. You don't see the outside world for days and everyone loses weight and doesn't eat properly. There is, however, a remarkable desire amongst most actors and people who work in the theatre to put in a twelve-hour day and then go down the pub. Especially when that pub is full of other actors and bouncing Brazilians having a laugh with a drum. But then you're up the next morning, plucking your tongue from the carpet, and you're working at full tilt. Usually with a sword.

I remember after one of these nights, the first thing I had to do in the morning, was strap a sword in a harness to my back, in full costume, and go right up to the top of the theatre and get on a ladder and be lowered in. No matter how much I had done it in The Swan way back in 2000, I was very unused to that sort of height now. More so after a night full of sambas and a head like an anvil. It's very high up there and we had to work out an entire routine where I would be clipped on for safety, first to the grid and then to the ladder. Believe you me, when you have to step on to that ladder which is just hanging in empty space, fifty feet up, it's no joke. And then, of course, you end up clinging on to that damn thing for hours, because they're not ready down below. You're sweating, fearing for your life and Chris has just trodden on your hand as he's tried to get on the ladder too. Then suddenly you're lowered in and do the scene and someone cries out 'Stop!' for some little technicality and you just say to yourself 'Please, don't', but then sure enough you are left there, stuck in mid-air, and the cheese grater of a harness is exploring places you never knew existed. I was up there for the whole day whilst we worked on that scene. Boy, did I need a pint after that...

After three or four days, the time comes to put the show on for the first time in front of an audience. This is the time. This is the moment, and I still get nervous just thinking about it now. Am I going to remember all my lines? What about the fights? Am I going to plunge horribly to my death from the top of this crazily high theatre as I ponce about with a sword on a ladder? Are we going to be OK? All the anxieties, insecurities, fears, hopes and joys that performing in front of an audience can bring. This time, of course, it was complicated by the fact that the theatre was still being built and no-one had ever worked in it before so we'd been delayed. We hadn't had a Dress Rehearsal and we were, literally, flying by the seat of our pants.

But it was such a big moment to be doing the first show in this very special theatre that we could only hoist up our trousers and go for it. Michael said a few words to the audience along the lines of 'we don't know how this going to pan out but stick with us' and offered them a free drink in the interval, and as we stood backstage hugging and wishing each other luck, I realised how this was the real start of our very long journey. Over the next two years we were going to open seven more shows and go through all manner of hoops, swings and roundabouts. I felt incredibly excited about it. What else could you want to do in life? The incense and smoke began to rise and swish amongst us. The funeral drums began to beat; I could hear the girls, placed around the auditorium, begin to wail; and the lads in front of me, all swords and ceremony, pushed open the doors of the tower and marched away to lower in the coffin. I followed them out and my heart was bursting with pride. It went without a hitch.

After the initial slog of getting the three shows on, it was now time to fine-tune during the period of 'previews' before the official opening of the show: the 'Press Night', as it's called. Now the day is extended from ten in the morning to doing a show at night as well, so that means leaving the theatre at about 11 o'clock at night. And then back in the next day. This whole period, of course, was elongated because we were putting on THREE shows.

Each day there would be cuts and additions, tweaks and tuning. For example, a cage covered in roses, from which we could pick in the Temple Garden scene and which would then be lowered to become Mortimer's prison in *Part I*, was cut after just one performance. This was replaced by a circular bower of red and white roses spiralling up to the gods, but that was thrown out and ended up hanging in the foyer for the next two years. We settled in the end on single roses suspended on wire lines. Simple, but a lot more effective. The audience could see us for a start. And we could see them. Which is the idea. Theatre should be a transformative experience for audience and actors alike, achieved through collaboration and communication. As actors in this show we were lost if two actors just played the scene to themselves. There is an audience out there! Actors are sometimes quite good at forgetting this, largely through years of playing on 'proscenium arch' theatres where they can't see the audience and the audience are watching nice pretty pictures and can barely see the actors because they're so far away. In my view it can be boring and exclusive, and no wonder no one goes anymore. Our job in these shows was to let the audience in. A play is not called a 'play' for nothing. It is the reason the stage is built into the body of the auditorium, where we play *with* the audience and from there take them on a journey.

And what a long journey it was. Our first 'Trilogy Day' was a big one for us all. It is such a big day of performance. All three Parts of *Henry VI* in one day – and even though I had done these before five years ago, it was still a huge shock to the system. In at nine in the morning for Fight Calls, Rope Calls, Make-up and Wig Calls, then perform till eleven at night. I remember reaching about 9 o'clock in the evening, when I first looked at the clock. A wave of tiredness had swept over me, and I couldn't believe it was dark again so soon. The whole day had gone and I was exhausted, but I still had to go on as Young Somerset in *Part III* and give it large with fighting and general gung-ho. Then, after my final exit, a huge rush of pride and relief accompanied by a mad dash round to watch the last ten minutes of the show to see how the others were getting on and then take the curtain call. The piled ranks of the audience who, let us not forget, had been sitting all day and been just as much a character in the plays as us, rose as one to give a standing ovation which reduced most of the exhausted, emotional cast to tears.

Finally we 'opened' the shows with another Trilogy day a week or so later. For the rest of that summer we played, literally. Mine and Clive's place in Waterside was host to a fair few histories itself, and all the while, after the opening Press Night, we were doing understudy rehearsals by day and performing by night.

The RSC has a policy of staging 'Understudy Runs' with full technical support for every show they do, so the actors can be as prepared as they can if they ever have to take the place of another actor. It is something very necessary, but when you are performing a completely different character by night, it is so ridiculously tiring it's almost funny. All the lines have been learnt in initial rehearsals, but in this job you had to keep them fresh over the course of two years, faced with the possibility of never having to use them, but they had to be there. Just under half of the cast over the course of two and a half years were 'off' – ill or indisposed – at one time or another, which meant you had to be on your toes in case anybody went down and you were thrown on. It's tough and bowel-loosening, but part of the job.

As the willows yellowed on the river, we left Stratford and hit the heady delights of Clapham once more, this time to rehearse the sequel: *Richard III*. Others now had a chance to pick up the baton. Hannah Barrie, for example, who for the whole summer had been playing various witches, gentlewomen and nurses, now got the chance to spread her wings as Lady Anne in *Richard III*. So too Ann Ogbomo as Elizabeth. I got to prance around with Keith Dunphy as a pair of bespectacled murderers trying to kill Jimmy Tucker as the Duke of Clarence. And we all rallied round Jonathan Slinger, playing Richard, as he faced learning and portraying one of the biggest roles in Shakespeare.

We decided that in order fully to explore the 'History' of these History Plays, we would look at them through the prism of the time in which they were set (medieval); the time when they were written (Elizabethan); and the time in which they were staged (modern). Within this context, we felt *Richard III* – with its sense of menace and state control – could lend itself to being explored and told through a modern slant. This is a sequel of course, so all the people still surviving from the bloody carnage of the previous plays would still play the same parts. But from gowns and broadswords, now it was all suits and guns, SWAT teams and sunglasses.

We'd been together for nine months and rehearsals were a joy. We were singing from the same hymn sheet and could explore things with a passion and commitment not possible had we just come together for that one play. Before we left for a couple of days off over Christmas we stood around the piano and sang carols and opened presents for each other. We had become a family.

The New Year dawned and we arrived back in Stratford to stage *Richard III* and then remount the summer's *Henry VI Parts I, II & III*. Once or twice we had taken a morning to run through a *Part* or two, so the lines were still fresh. Ish. But you dust them off pretty quickly when you have a day's Tech for each one then go straight into perform-

ing all four at once. *Part One* on a Friday night. The other two *Parts*
Saturday morning and afternoon, *Richard III* in the evening. Wow.

This time next year we would be re-rehearsing these plays, having
spent the whole year rehearsing and performing their prequels,
Richard II, *Henry IV Parts I & II* and *Henry V*, in preparation for staging
all eight plays at once. We would end up performing all this in a 'Glorious Moment' by staging *Richard II* on a Thursday night; *Henry IV Parts
I & II* and *Henry V* as a trilogy day on the Friday; another Trilogy the
next day with *Henry VI Parts I, II & III* on the Saturday; with *Richard III*
on the Sunday afternoon.

WHAT????!!!!

Two trilogy days back-to-back? Eight shows? All the understudy
stuff? The lines. THE LINES? How many were there? And, what's
more, in London we would be repeating the same thing over a couple
of months! I just did not know how we were going to do it.

But this I did know: As we arrived back in Clapham a year to the week
after we started, and five more actors slipped seamlessly into the cast to
rehearse *Richard II* (this one to be in full Elizabethan costume), I knew
that I could not be in a better group of people, cast, crew and creative
team alike, to do something which had never been done before. To
scale this unclimbed summit.

And I knew I had to write about it. We had been through such an
extraordinary time already. A process which, in my experience, had
already involved the audience to an unprecedented degree. We had
garnered such levels of trust and faith in each other as a cast, and
with our audiences, that we could take whatever was thrown at us and
deliver it back with interest.

To write a Blog, for me, was merely an extension of that connection
with the audience and my colleagues. To perform, deliver the experience, tell the story, in as many ways as possible.

I still didn't know how we were going to do it, though.

The Histories Time Line

February to June 2006	Rehearse *Henry VI Parts I, II & III* in London
June to November 2006	Perform *Henry VI Parts I, II & III* in Stratford-upon-Avon
November 2006 to January 2007	Rehearse *Richard III* in London
January to February 2007	Perform *Richard III* and *Henry VI Parts I, II & III* in Stratford-upon-Avon
February to June 2007	Rehearse *Richard II, Henry IV Parts I & II* in London
June 2007	Blog starts
July to September 2007	Perform *Richard II, Henry IV Parts I & II* in Stratford-upon-Avon
September to October 2007	Rehearse *Henry V* in London
October 2007 to February 2008	Perform *Henry V* and *Richard II, Henry IV Parts I & II* in Stratford-upon-Avon
February to March 2008	Perform *Richard II, Henry IV Parts I & II, Henry V, Henry VI Parts I, II & III, Richard III* in Stratford-upon-Avon
April to May 2008	Perform *Richard II, Henry IV Parts I & II, Henry V, Henry VI Parts I, II & III, Richard III* in The Roundhouse, London
June 2008	Collapse

THE BLOG

SPRING 2007
LONDON

THERE are three rehearsal rooms at the RSC's building in Clapham. We, the Histories company, manage to use all three at the same time. Which is a bit mind-boggling when you have to come out of one room and leap straight into a different play and different character in another. Which King is it? Who's alive? Who did I kill? And who's he/she playing in this one? However, in the bottom room there's also a table tennis table.

This has been a fixture for the Histories for the last year and has been a life-saver. We got it when we all had a whip round and were organised by our chief self-appointed social organiser, Keith Bartlett, who plays Talbot in *Henry VI Part I* (seven year-old boy in a fifty year-old grizzled façade). It quickly became a focus for a lot of men who were thrown together for a very long time to bond and play. It was hugely successful. It even got to the point of whenever we had a break from rehearsals there would be a race to grab bats and get on before some other guy stole it. Katy Stephens restored order by whipping our hides at it, but then she does that sort of thing...

We still play but time is getting pressing as we are rehearsing three plays at once now. Geoffrey Streatfeild is very good – remaining unbeaten for weeks – and then Clive Wood upped his game and beat him in Stratford where we had the table backstage. I beat Clive, but then Bartlett (crafty) beat me. Patrice Naiambana is a wizard but was beaten by Streatfeild who regained his crown by edging past Clive in a nervy encounter after Clive had died in *Part III*. As it stands now, I, for only the second time, have beaten Streatfeild in a taut and tense five-setter, but then got whipped by Clive soon after. It's turning into a parody of the plays we are doing with one person on top and then another in quick succession...

We are all beginning to crank up for one last effort here in London after a four-month rehearsal process before the real work begins when we come to Stratford the first week of July. Michael Boyd is rehearsing *Richard II* and *Henry IV Part I* upstairs in the top room. Richard Twyman is rehearsing *Henry IV Part II* in the middle room. Donnacadh O'Briain is taking understudy rehearsals in the bottom room – when he can get us off the table tennis table.

Today I'm in to re-rehearse the death of Richard II in Act 5 of *Richard II*. Considering we first rehearsed this in March you might think we'd be getting tired of it by now, but yesterday I was rehearsing Act 2 Scene 4 of *Henry IV Part II* – a good five hours of stage time later. And about 20 years in History time…

But, strangely, none of this is confusing… I mean it. One of the wonderful things about this project is that, as performers, we are able to expand and take in huge amounts of information whilst PLAYING. And that's what it's all about in my book. And hopefully that sense of play and of joy in telling the story communicates itself to the audience and they enjoy and understand and love the experience as much as we do.

And we're also bloody good at playing at table tennis…

THINGS are beginning to hot up in time for our move back to Stratford in a week and half's time. (EEEK!). We were rehearsing *Richard II* Act 1 sc 1 yesterday morning. Then our first 'stagger' through, as opposed to a run through, of *Henry IV Part II*. It went well. We've still got plenty of work to do, and time is of the essence, but we've our noses to the grindstone.

19 June 2007

Considering *Henry IV Part II* is now our seventh play in The Histories it is amazing how together it all is. People are remembering most of their lines and everybody else's too: on top of a busy day today we have an Understudy Line Run of *Henry IV Part I* until 9.30 this evening. Another 12-hour day for some people. This means that because we're all understudying each other, and each have a play off within the eight History Plays we're doing, each person has the text and moves of 14 plays in their heads at any one time.

This is quite a lot of lines.

Some people are understudying sometimes three or four characters in one play so in the course of these two and a half years one person may have played up to twenty different characters. Which is fun. It's almost like rep. Which of course is what it is.

I was thinking during the stagger through yesterday and marvelling how differently we are working now. We've been together a year and a half, and rather like a football team that gels over the course of a season or two, so we have a language of working and ease with each other and an intuition that I find very inspiring.

Got fitted up for Bushy in *Richard II* and Pistol in *Henry IV Part II* today. Very exciting. I love it when the costumes start appearing. You can be a kid and start playing. The designers, makers, armourers and leather workers are into overdrive now. It's a weird feeling just standing there with your arms out, in your underwear, whilst about five people busy themselves around you measuring, pinning, looking askance at you as they try to imagine what it looks like, making decisions, pulling, yanking, pushing, laughing.

God, I love this job.

SUMMER 2007
STRATFORD-UPON-AVON

4 July 2007

WELL, it's lunchtime on our first day of Technical Rehearsals for *Richard II*. The circus has come to town and we're all itching to go. The Dirty Duck's takings have increased dramatically and we're all dressed in our Elizabethan finery for this one.

There's nothing like that first moment, as we had last night, when after so long rehearsing and imagining, everyone gets into their costume and starts playing. It's always so funny. I'm sure my costume's shrunk since I was measured for it a month or two ago. I suspect it might get bigger during the run. Last year, doing the *HenryVIs* I lost a stone and a half during the summer. Man, those costumes stank.

We've spent the morning getting the opening scene right. We all move in formation and everything has to be done with pinpoint accuracy. It's a really precise show compared to the bludgeoning force of the Henries last year – rapier rather than broadsword – so we have to be very disciplined. As Richard falls, so the broadswords start coming back and we can FIGHT MORE! What fun!

19 July 2007

IT'S the first day of tech for *Henry IV Part II* and as the rain comes down outside so I have thrown myself through another trap door inside The Courtyard. It's a tricky manoeuvre, and an act of trust, to go head first into a trap and hope that someone hasn't whipped away the crash mat. But fun anyway.

The first four previews of *Richard II* came in a flash. The first night felt so good to be let off the leash and performing again for all of us, but we were all shaking with nerves. It's such a specific show that you've got to be right on the money from the start. And we pulled it off. Just.

It's at times like these that I get all weepy about this company of actors, directors, designers, costume and wigs, props, fly and stage staff. Everyone's putting in 12-hour days at least to get these three shows on and, we, the actors, take all the applause. But there are so many who are working so hard to fling this thing on. It's thrilling.

I've had *Henry IV Part I* off. A weird experience. Going to see it on Tuesday night was brilliant. I kept on wanting to jump out of my seat and say, 'This is the bit where I come on', but I just sat there bursting with pride instead. Over the last year and a half we have spent the majority of our lives together in one way or another, and to see a snapshot of what the audience experience was exhilarating.

And now *Part II* arrives. We rehearse this afternoon. Start Technical rehearsals this evening. The production team have a strange ethereal look about them and look vaguely grey. But the theatre lights do a great job of making them appear normal. The actors have all got sprightly after an unaccustomed morning off. And I happened to wander in early and immediately got told to throw myself into the stage.

Could be worse.

W E'RE now back onto *Richard II* after having put on *Henry IV Part II* all last week. Man, that was a tough week.

It's a very complicated and hard show to get right and we're getting there. Everyone is knackered. We've had more 'notes' – the thoughts and suggestions Michael gives us through sitting us all down in a session with our pens and paper at the ready – than a piano. We've been in re-rehearsals all day every day and then performing in the evening.

Returning to *Richard II*, however, was a joy. We really got a lick on it and came out all guns blazing and, I don't know what the audience thought, but I came off stage buzzing. Which warranted a couple in the Duck afterwards, I felt.

The opening preview of *Henry IV Part II* was another thrilling little number. A good few underpants were put to the test again, I'm sure. It felt a little by the seat of our pants too, but we did it and had a great time... Some of us were a bit ill. I was bent double with stomach pains all show. No drink in the Duck that night. But by Friday we were all fine and back on all cylinders.

I had a lump on my head all day on Saturday, because I got hit on the head with a bottle.

I must stress that this was during the show. As part of the desire to get the drunken Pistol off stage, we've devised a whole routine where I, as Pistol, stagger about a bit after my fight with Falstaff and then Bardolph whacks me over the head with a bottle, whereupon I fall, prostrate and unconscious, through a trapdoor. The bottle is made of sugar glass and is usually utterly painless as it shatters. But you have to get it just right. I was a smidgeon out of position and it gave me a fearful

whack. Which warranted another couple in the Duck,
I felt.

Tonight it's *Richard II* again. We had a rehearsal
this morning of Act 2 sc 4 of *Henry IV Part II* and then
rehearsing all afternoon for tonight so you have to get
your head round a pretty big landscape.

Which might lead to ANOTHER couple in the Duck,
but let's see how the show goes...

I T'S August 2nd, my dear late father's birthday, and
I've had two days off.

2 August 2007

Which, frankly, I didn't know what to do with. I'm
not in *Henry IV Part I* so it feels like I was put on the
bench whilst the rest of the team went out and played.
It's strange because whilst we all really appreciate the
time off, we are operating at such a high pitch that I
feel as though I'm straining at the leash when sitting
at home relaxing. Still, it gave me a chance to finish
Harry Potter.

And what's more I'm gunning to get back to Pistol
tonight. We've just been rehearsing Act 2 sc 4 this
morning. I nearly took off Chris McGill's head like the
top of a boiled egg as he stands in one of the traps and
I wave my sword around. He shot down the trap like a
Jack-in-a-box in reverse. Michael liked it so much that
we kept it in. We had to work on that one to get it right.

One of the great things about this whole project
is the odd situations you find yourself in. The area
underneath the stage, or 'sub-stage' as it's called,
provides access to and from the trapdoors on stage and
to various technical wizardry that lies beneath like
smoke machines, lights and speakers, and is only about

three feet high. You have to crawl around down there. Which, with a sword and a long coat, is easier said than done. The areas below each trap are boxed off to form their own little performance area, where Julius D'Silva and Wela Frasier and I found ourselves laying flat on our backs on a crash mat underneath the main upstage trap waiting to make our entrance. They kept stopping up above as they rehearsed the scene, so we were there for nearly an hour, cooped up in the dark, in a space no bigger than a double bed. It was like a scene from *The Great Escape*. By the end we just started laughing and laughing as you do when things get silly. And then suddenly we flung ourselves out and we were off. Throwing ourselves about the stage, laughing, fighting, shouting and whispering. Working. Finding out how we can do it better. Each crease and fold in this almighty tapestry we are weaving sewn and unpicked and sewn again.

Warmth. Such warmth.

I've just had two days off – it's right to be rosy. And it's my dear Dad's birthday. Would've been 76. So I'm allowed to be lyrical. Worth a toast and a couple in the Duck at least…

8 August 2007

WHOAH, these are the hard yards.

We did a show of *Richard II* last night. We hadn't performed it for 8 days so it was interesting bumping into the lines again. We've been working so hard on the other plays that it's always something of a shock to find yourself deep into *Richard II* territory.

Exhausted after the show to find we had another twelve-hour day today. Notes, and working on scenes

from all three plays. They're working on *Part I* as I
write so I've half an hour off. Then we have a show this
evening and then we're in at 9.15 tomorrow morning
for our first Trilogy Day of these three particular plays.
We're all in anticipation and shock in equal measure.
Poor Clive, who's in all three with a lot to do, drags
himself from one note session to another and to the
dressing room, collapsing in a heap. We have noticed
the sun has come out, and we grab it in our little
enclosure out the back whenever we can.

I know this sounds like some form of boot camp, but it
isn't – it's just bloody hard work. Let's face it, doing just
one play after this is going to be a doddle. We are all still
up for the shows and totally committed to the work.
And we are here to play. As are all the technical team
who are working just as hard, if not harder. I don't know
how Michael does it all and manages to run the whole
RSC at the same time. But then he's a freak.

Deep breath, it's a trilogy day tomorrow. Not too
many in the Duck tonight, I fear.

I T'S Tuesday and we're on the final run in towards
press day and then a two week break. Last
Thursday – the Trilogy Day – was a tough one but I
think we were all elated at the end of it.

All the Trilogy virgins, and David Warner as Falstaff
especially, got so much out of it. That's the beauty
of doing something like three shows in one day. The
audience are with you on the arc of your character's
journey: so the stuff that Clive Wood, say, was doing by
the end of *Henry IV Part II* in the evening, compared

14 August 2007

to the same character that we see in the first scene of
Richard II way back in the morning, has so much more
impact on an audience that has witnessed it all. The
same goes for David as Falstaff, Geoff as Hal, Kieran as
Poins, indeed us all. Even with a play off in the middle,
you could sense from the audience in *Part II* the feeling
they were recognising old friends from *Richard II*.

Friday was a long struggle after that. I've been doing
Trilogy days on and off for 7 years now and I've never
known them to schedule in a performance the day after.
I don't know how that slipped through the net.

We had an interesting day on Saturday when David was
taken ill in the afternoon. Julius, his understudy, then
had to go on. It was a big moment and we all rallied
round. We got through, and it is a testament to the
deep value and trust we place in each other, and the
never-say-die spirit, that we pulled it off. David is back
now, all guns blazing, and we're ready for the Press Day.
Although, I personally never know why anyone gets
het-up about these things. It's a day to mark the opening
of it all. But that's all it is. It's only the press. And
nobody died so let's get on with it…

At least, that's what I'm telling myself.

18 August 2007   WHAT a great day it turned out to be!
        The Press Day Trilogy went as smoothly as
could be expected. In fact better. Cordery has written
something in the programme about the amount
of adrenalin going through an actor's body on first
night being enough to kill a man. With our combined
adrenalin at 10.30 that morning I'm sure we could have

felled an army – which is of course what we do through
most of these plays...

Right from the opening staged dance of *Richard II* –
the Pavanne Blob – it began really to kick off. Act 1 sc 1
of *Richard II* was firing and we took it from there. Some
of us, of course, had a play off and I for one found it
really difficult to relax knowing that friends were busy
out there giving it large. *Part II* came and I shot off as
Pistol. What fun. Then suddenly it was the curtain call.
What a fantastic reaction and we, audience and cast
alike, felt really part of a whole. Of something. Of a wee
bit of joy.

My Dad would have loved it all, and in a way, I'm
sure he did. My brother was in and a teacher, Colin
Gray, who first got me to do acting when he cast me
as Benedick at school in *Much Ado About Nothing* a
LONG time ago. It was great to share it all with them,
and we knocked back a few glasses at the after show
party. Everyone seemed thrilled and exhausted in equal
measure. Then it was down the Duck for a few pints
and a dance.

So many faces and so many smiles.

Finally, a day off yesterday. Spent nursing myself
and frantically scrabbling around a drawer for some
paracetamol, but mostly in a not unpleasant haze. Cast
outing to see *The Bourne Ultimatum*. Normally, the last
thing you want to do on a night off is go into a theatre
or cinema, but given the weather and our addled brains,
it was a joy.

Just one more show to do tonight – the afternoon show
of *Henry IV Part I* was another joy apparently – and
then we go on holiday for two weeks. It seems strange
to break just as we've opened but we will get plenty of
chance to run them in over the winter. We have the

small matter of rehearsing *Henry V* to come. Weirdly, I'm looking forward to it. These have been some of the hardest six weeks I have ever known in the theatre. We are emotionally and physically drained. The holiday will do us good and then roll on *Henry V*. It's the last play and we're going to give it everything we've got.

AUTUMN 2007
LONDON

5 September 2007

WHAT a difference a couple of weeks makes! After a two-week holiday we all met up back at the Clapham rehearsal rooms with big smiles on our faces, hugging each other (it's all very touchy-feely this acting lark), and looking ten years younger. We really do. People's eyes are bright. We are shaven. We are not walking out into natural light blinking and shaking like released hostages. We have energy. We can remember the names of our families and friends.

Holidays. One of the (many) extraordinary things about this project is the concept of holidays. I've only ever had one proper holiday since I left college. Most of the time as an actor you don't know where your next job is coming from and so you can only really 'have a holiday' if, conversely, you know you have work coming up. But to have a properly defined two-week period where you're still getting paid and you can genuinely relax is still quite a novel experience for me.

One of the least talked-about notions of ensemble, in all the discussions the RSC and others are having, is the simple one that an actor surely does better when he doesn't have the threat of penury hanging, scythe-like, above his or her head. They can relax and start to give a true account of their work and talent. The counter argument to this is that if you don't have that threat then you become complacent and idle. This is, of course, utter nonsense. As someone who has spent the best part of 12 years hiding from bank managers and playing Russian Roulette with cash machines, I can safely report that it is MUCH better to be where I am now.

Which is back rehearsing with a fully reinvigorated director and cast. I feel as though we're really going to be let off the leash on this *Henry V*, the eighth and last of our plays. We know each other so well, and, as Michael said on Monday, we will know most of our audience so well by the time we finally put this one on that we need to celebrate that too.

I think we're going to go out with a bang! Still, there's a lot of hard work to do before that. And if all goes to plan we've got another year left yet...

D EEP and dark into rehearsals for *Henry V*. Monday morning, fresh from a weekend of slavish devotion to line learning. Honest. Well, a few lines followed by the hoovering. Followed by cleaning the kitchen floor, recounting the lines. Followed by a few more lines and the windows are now sparkling. This line-learning thing is very good for boring chores as it allows me to go through them whilst not getting distracted elsewhere. That is, of course, until the call of the wild hits and I bolt for a bottle of wine. Nothing seems to stay in the head much after that. Believe me, I've tried.

Then you come into rehearsals on a Monday morning confident you've done your homework, you open your mouth and you speak drivel. It's really quite astonishing. You make passable impersonations of a drowning man, all hope is lost, and any stock you had with the director is as worthwhile as Northern Rock...

Other than that, I think it's all going very well.

17 September 2007

This was the week of the run on Northern Rock bank, when its customers queued to get their money out before it went bust.

I WORKED it out, in a rather black mood on the bus this morning, that in this 28-month project we spend 13 of them rehearsing in London.

That, dear reader, is a long time to spend in Clapham. As we rehearse, the gentle sounds of police sirens accompany our lilting iambics. The floor rumbles and shakes every time a tube train passes underneath. Car alarms seem to greet each quiet passage of intimate acting with unerring accuracy. During the summer it was hot and we had the fire escape doors open, and a drunk wandered in only to be greeted by me in full flow as Pistol waving a machete. He seemed to recognise a kindred spirit, gave me and the scurrying stage management a respectful nod, turned tail, and staggered off into the day.

I was rehearsing a fight at about half past eight in the evening last year and we heard gunshots outside. What with the clanking of swords we were generating inside, it was like a scene from *Highlander*. The HSBC at the top of the road had a little spot of bother with an armed robbery last week – the second time that's happened this year. And, worse, the Railway Tavern across the road doesn't sell real ale.

The worse times, such as today, are when you're in at 10 and work hard all morning on a scene. Then you have to hang around, as I have to do today, until 7.30 to rehearse a scene till 9 o'clock. This may sound like the petty whinge of a spoilt actor, which, frankly, it is, but I'd rather be working flat out, not be put on hold. Because you can't go anywhere. You can't plan because you might get called back in, or the 7.30 call might never happen because we've overrun. It's inevitable given the way we're working, but I find these days more of a grind than working flat out all day for 13 hours.

Having said that, I don't know how Michael does it. The levels of concentration and commitment to the work he has seem bottomless, and he's the one in there all day every day.

But we have a show to put on and we're all throwing everything at it. So, mustn't grumble. And, as the sirens pelt by and the trains rumble on, we can console ourselves that we've only another 4 weeks till we start tech rehearsals in Stratford. FOUR WEEKS!!!! EEK!! ONLY FOUR WEEKS! Better stop writing and go learn my lines and use my time properly instead of whingeing.

13 months? We need more time…!

I T'S half past four on a Monday afternoon and I've just been sacked. 24 September 2007

Before the protest marchers begin to form, let me explain: from a scene. I've just spent the best part of two days rehearsing a scene in which Pistol officially doesn't appear, but Michael thought it'd be interesting if I were to be there in the background. We started our usual routine of work. We all read the scene aloud together. Then went through it line by line with a fine toothcomb, extracting our story from it all and discussing and playing. This was Friday. Then this morning we did more of the same and into another scene. Then it was time to put it on its feet and see what we came up with. Two goes through and Michael says to me, hmmm, not so sure you work in this. It's distracting. You're sacked. Which is nice. But, frankly, he's right.

Still, I got to know a bit more about the play and I always find it fascinating to be in on scenes when you're not actually in them yourself. It gives a better snapshot of what others are doing.

Streatfeild and I have started up a rather mean game of cricket using a tennis ball and a sword. (In the absence of Keith Bartlett, who has this play off, the table tennis bats have been left up in Stratford and nobody's quite organised enough to get them back apart from Keith). Luke Neal is a novice left-hander but he's the size of bull which means that when he connects, everyone hits the deck and the windows are threatened. Rob Carroll is a brutal Aussie bowler (what would you expect?). A glorious On-drive from Geoffrey very nearly took out John Woolf, the RSC's Head of Music, sitting foolishly at Mid On having a chat.

Other than that things are going along nicely. Although I have to say Michael does look faintly mystified when returning from a lunch break to be greeted by a communal cry of HOWZAT!?!

And, even though I was sacked, I thought it was Not Out...

28 September 2007

LEEKS. And more leeks. Raw leeks.
    It's Friday, early evening, and I've spent all day rehearsing and most of the afternoon getting a raw leek shoved down my mouth by Jon Slinger. Not a job for the inexperienced. His character in this play, Fluellen, is a particularly anal Welshman who tires of Pistol's continual racism against the Welsh and eventually

has his revenge by force-feeding Pistol with a leek and generally giving him a good beating.

I suppose that I will eat more leeks now in rehearsal than when we're actually doing the show, but I can tell you already that my attitude is shifting towards the things. Cheesy leeks are not going to be top of my menu for quite some time I fear.

The rest of the show is coming on apace. I think it's shaping up nicely. We suddenly realised a couple of days ago that the initial period of rehearsal that we always do, which consists of minutely going through the text and discussing so that we're all beginning to sing from the same hymn sheet, so to speak, was over and everything was on its feet – in whatever shaky form – for the last time in this great project. Strange to think that we won't be going back and starting a play. However, I think we've got quite enough to be looking forward to. The staging of *Henry V*. The re-staging of *Richard II*, *Henry IV Parts I & II*. Then the re-staging of the *Henry VIs* and *Richard III*. Then putting them all on together. Plus all the understudy work for each play. Then the mounting in London of them all.

Yes, we've enough to keep us busy.

And all the while, if today is anything to go by, I shall smell faintly of leek.

I T'S Day 575 in The RSC House. Roughly. And Nick is sitting in the corner in a quiet moment, musing over his sword, counting the days backwards.

This project sometimes does feel like *Big Brother* when the press turn up and hang about in the rehearsal

4 October 2007

rooms to do some article (like they did last year when Michael described us as a 'right bunch of nutters') or when we do the Press Nights and the reviews come out. It would, of course, be a lot more interesting than *Big Brother*. We've got swords for a start. And we ARE a bunch of nutters. And I love every single one of 'em.

We were all dragged in this morning to try and stage the end of the siege of Harfleur. About six or seven goes through (poor Geoffrey: having to summon up the big 'How yet resolves the Governor of the town?' speech from his boots every time) and we were all sacked again. Cue much pointed packing of bags.

But this is what we have to do. We are experimenting in ways we could never have dreamt of when this project began. The simple act of having twenty or so blokes all crowded around first the galleries and then on stage; then cheering offstage; then quietly coming on at the end, was a process whereby Michael and Geoffrey could experiment with the power that 'army' presence brings to the speech. The fact that we're all now cut from the scene doesn't matter as it will immeasurably help Geoffrey in his mind that his tired and bedraggled army ARE there. And thence of course the audience will feel that they are there too. And you never know, Michael might bring us all in once we get to the theatre.

Tired and bedraggled is a fairly apt phrase for most of us at the moment. Well, me anyway. I've a filthy cold and because I no longer live in London, I'm sleeping on various mates' floors, sofas and spare beds whilst we rehearse. I'm immensely grateful but there are times, especially with a runny nose and a head that feels like a slurry pit, when you just want your own bed. I keep on getting leeks shoved down my gob by Jon Slinger (he

just won't stop) and there are plenty of scenes where I
don't have the faintest idea of what I'm doing.

I'm loving it.

Roll on Day 576...

Oh, and my little nephew Samuel William Stuart
Asbury was born this morning! His middle two names
are my late father's names. My big brother is little
Samuel's father. I am immeasurably proud. And he's a
much better Big Brother than the one on TV.

WELL, it's Tuesday and thoughts naturally stray
towards the big day on Saturday...

After a sluggish start and an enforced back to the wall
situation from very early on in the campaign England
finally take on France in a crucial decider.

After sterling work in the last 3 games Rob
'MacMorris' Carrol keeps his place in the front row
alongside Forbes 'Chorus' Masson at Hooker and Clive
'Daddy' Wood, who again retains his place at loose-head
despite not training with the team for the last 6 weeks
claiming exhaustion.

In the power house second row Luke 'Gloucester'
Neal and Tom 'Westmoreland' Hodgkins renew their
successful partnership from the previous match. Paul
'Gower' Williams, Patrice 'Warwick' Naiambana and
Julius 'Bardolph' D'Silva comprise a formidable back
row blending the experience and solidity of Hamilton
with the fiery Naiambana and the hard-hitting D'Silva.

Jon 'Fluellen' Slinger wins his place at scrum-
half alongside playmaker Geoffrey 'Hal' Streatfeild

9 October 2007

*In the Rugby World
Cup 2007, England
unexpectedly reach
the semi-finals, where
they are to meet a
strong French team
in Paris. This has
certain resonances...*

at outside-half. An untested combination, each have shone individually in the past, but Head Coach Michael Boyd said: 'In practice and various training drills, they've shown a remarkable empathy with one another.' It remains to be seen whether specialist backs coach Roger Watkins agrees, although it will be his job to oversee that the growing understanding between Nick 'Pistol' Asbury at inside centre and Lex 'Williams' Shrapnel, at outside centre, continues to prosper.

With the ever dependable Chris 'Bedford' McGill flying up the right wing and the young but talented Wela 'Peto' Frasier on the left it will be Asbury and Shrapnel's job to get it to these boys as quickly as possible with the full back Miles 'Exeter' Richardson, who will be winning his fiftieth cap, coming into the line and punching a hole wherever possible. The newly minted captain Streatfeild is not expected to use his formidable kicking attributes but has been told by Boyd and Watkins to play a passing game. Although with Slinger finding those probing little gaps in and around the contact area and Hamilton on hand to pick up any scraps, the battle may well be fought in midfield with high balls aplenty and Frasier and McGill ready to run on to them.

Whilst speculation runs high in the press of Streatfeild and Alexia 'French Kate' Healy's impending marriage and how this could effect both sides, Nick 'Pistol' Asbury is reportedly distraught at the news from England that his wife Maureen 'Nell' Beattie is very ill back at home of the Malady of France.

The French line up is as expected with Sandy 'King of France' Neilson naming an unchanged side. At fly-half John 'Dauphin' Mackay will be providing his touches of flair, whilst the sensation in the last two games, Kieran 'Orleans' Hill, at flanker will prove a tough proposition for the likes of Shrapnel and Asbury in midfield. Jimmy

'Scroop' Tucker, having left the English camp earlier in the year and now qualifying for France controversially, will be looking to settle a few scores on the wing where it will be an interesting tussle between the light toes of McGill and the dancing feet of Tucker.

The seasoned Anthony 'Constable' Bunsee at full-back will be challenged under the high ball of Streatfeild but in his last two outings was able to offload in the contact area with impunity. Matt 'Bastard' Costain at scrum-half will swing high and low to scrabble for any loose ball at the back of the scrum where Slinger's efforts will be threatened also by Anthony 'Cambridge' Shuster (another defector from the great schism early in the year at the training ground in Southampton) who will be certain to re-establish his credentials as a flanker with great ball-handling skills.

Sources from within the French camp report a worrying insouciance, believing all they have to do is turn up and they will win on Saturday. And, frankly, who can disagree. Their strength in numbers at the contact area will, I fear, be too strong. Indeed, Streatfeild himself warned 'It is true, we are in great danger' and exhorted his troops to 'summon up the blood'. Keith 'Nym' Dunphy pulled up with a stiffened sinew, but is reported to be back to full training.

But can this band of brothers succeed? With Keith 'Talbot' Bartlett as forwards coach for the second year running, their tactics should be strong, but as Boyd pointed out in his latest post match interview:

'We must dare to fail.'

WE had our first 'Stagger' through yesterday of the whole caboodle. And, you know what, it wasn't that bad. In fact some of it – namely the scenes I'm not in – was brilliant.

Geoffrey, as Henry, excelled himself; Slinger's Welsh is really singing and getting a good bit of Merthyr into it; Geoff Freshwater reduced us to tears of laughter in the second scene, as did Hannah and Alexia, as Alice and Kate, later; and the reading out of the dead simply reduced me to tears.

As a consequence of all that I have a humdinger of a hangover and I still reek of leek. (Which sounds like something Jamie Oliver would cook...)

We have a week and a half to go before we move up to Stratford and start our week of tech rehearsals. This is where the real work starts. We've been working so hard already, but now we have something resembling a show, this is the time we put our foot on the gas and knock what we have in to shape. We are facing a Week of the Long Knives as there will be a fair degree of pruning: The great 'Cutting Of The Text We Have All Spent Hours Learning' ritual. But we've grown used to that.

And we had a nice evening in the pub afterwards and people who were doing understudy rehearsals long into the night came out and joined us. I have a vague recollection of ringing my mother later on. Which is strange. Never drunkenly done that before. And, frankly, a schoolboy error. 'Bout time I got a girlfriend again, by the sound of it. Sigh. But they wouldn't be able to put up with the smell of leek.

And then I had my second 'stagger through' of the day into my mate's flat. Thank God that wasn't a 'run' through. He wouldn't have been happy.

S ATURDAY morning we had rehearsals for
Henry V. In the afternoon we did a run of *Richard II*. THEN THERE WAS THE RUGBY. In which an underrated and underpowered English team beat a strongly fancied French team. Extraordinary. I'd love to say it was History repeating itself – sport as a representation of war and all that – but it's not of course. But we are in a History Cycle, and it's just our story that we're dealing with in *Henry V* at the moment, so the head, as well as History, starts to spin.

Geoffrey added to the piece I wrote about the rugby last week by recording the 'we few, we happy few...' speech for ITV which was played on the telly before the semi-final of the Rugby World Cup between England and France, and apparently in the England dressing room beforehand. So we like to think we had a hand in the win on Saturday night... Amazing what a bunch of namby-pamby actors can do!

A whole day off on Sunday! Then a run through of *Henry IV Parts I* and *II* on Monday. Then back to *Henry V* on Tuesday. Honestly, we're getting a little schizophrenic.

The runs of Richard and the Henries were fun affairs, not having done them for months. There is a strange feeling that comes over you when doing these things because your brain and your body act before you have time to think. Muscle memory and word memory beat thought, and you find yourself speaking, moving, dancing whilst in an almost out-of-body experience. The dance that Hannah, Anthony and I do as the Queen, Green and Bushy in *Richard II* we had not practised or gone through in 2 and half months and suddenly there it was. My feet seemed to be moving in the right places and my mouth was opening and closing but I had no knowledge of the moves or words. They were just there. And nobody seemed to stop me or giggle in the corner and hide their faces in bafflement, so I must've been doing roughly the right things.

Henry IV Part II was a more interesting affair because it was the least bedded-in of all the shows over the summer so some of the cuts etc were not as fresh in the mind as they might be. Still, we got through it. I couldn't remember half of my cuts and changes but we navigated around them… Sigh.

Then it was back to *Henry V*. We really are enjoying rehearsing this one. It's bloody hard work. And it's hard to get it right too. Pistol is a fascinating, weird, fantastic shambles of a character and I love him, but he's bloody difficult. Still, he'll be rewarding to play and hopefully the audience will go on that journey with him.

Which is of course what we have done with the England rugby team over the last few months! The final next. ONCE MORE UNTO THE BREECH, DEAR FRIENDS, ONCE MORE!!!!

19 October 2007

In the Rugby World Cup England had made it into the Final against South Africa. (They lost.)

IT'S Friday and tomorrow we have a final run in the morning and then we officially travel to Stratford from this dump in Clapham in the afternoon. WAHEY!

Today we have a second run through in the morning and afternoon, then notes. So it's all go. The mood in the camp is of high excitement. And that's not just because of the rugby. We're all loving doing this show, I think. I am, certainly. The rehearsals are hard, but the more you put in and all that…

Michael's really pushing me in this one. It's good, I need it. Getting me to try different things, to push the envelope. One thing he's really encouraging is Pistol's

relationship with the audience and he exhorts me to
try and 'give it out' to them more and more. Which
is all very well and good, but in the rehearsal room
that gets trickier and trickier, as all we have is some
rather gloomy dusty walls and six of your colleagues
standing around scratching their arses and waiting for
their entrance. Which isn't strictly true, as the support
and faith that this company (including all the stage
management and designers etc) give one another when
they're on the floor of the rehearsal room is something
very special and unique in my experience. But it's still
tricky when you have to 'talk to the audience' and it's a
mate looking back at you trying to maintain eye contact
and not make either side feel awkward.

Roll on the audience!

It should be a goody.

And I shan't be sad to see the back of Clapham.

WINTER 2007/08
STRATFORD-UPON-AVON

24 October 2007

TECHING.

We're back in Stratford, it's Wednesday morning and we're creeping along getting the show up. It's a long old process. This is a complicated show with lots of flying and things coming out of traps so it's all got to be minutely planned out. It takes a while and it's very laborious.

Having said all that, this has been the nicest tech I've ever been involved in. It's not just because of the company of actors that has been together for so long, it is the whole backstage crew, stage management and creative team. All the many very talented people who have worked so hard to bring these eight shows to life. As a consequence, having worked together so intensely for so long, we all know and have a confidence in each other so share a trust that you cannot buy.

We play. A play is not called a play for nothing. We are the 'flat, unraised, spirits that have dared / On this unworthy scaffold to bring forth / So great an object...'.

And it's great fun. It's going a bit slowly and we might not get a Dress in, but we're still enjoying it. There are a few sequences in this show where quite a lot of us – the English army in fact – spend a lot of time down underneath the stage waiting to come on out of the trapdoors. During show time we would only be there for a couple of minutes waiting to go, but in a tech we're there for ages whilst all gets technically plotted in around us. This, of course, leads to all sorts of ribaldry. It's like some boy scout camp after the teacher has told everyone to get to sleep in their tents. It's pitch black down there and there's lots of giggling and hitting and farting in the dark. And more giggling. Which gets slightly more insane the more we sit in there for a few hours. And I tell you, when you're lying down there – there's only three feet of headroom – with Patrice

Naiambana and his two swords, Katy Stephens covered in blood and Streatfeild snagging his crown in her hair, things are only going to get funnier…

W ELL it's half past six and we go up in an hour. AAAAAAAAAAAAAARRRGGHHH!!!!!

We were still teching Act 5 sc 1 at half past five this afternoon when we had to stop in order to do our first performance of this crazy show, *Henry V*, at half past seven. So we are flying by the seat of our pants. Wow. This is going to be a rollercoaster ride. The nerves and adrenalin are kicking in. People are pacing around talking to themselves and time has stood still. And quickened up.

Here we go. Blimey. Wish us luck.

I T'S Monday and we have now done three shows of *Henry V*.

Thursday went really well! PHEW!! It was a close run thing and we were really winging some of it but we all enjoyed it. In fact, it is on such moments that this company is based. We all worked for each other. We supported Geoffrey as Henry and he did us proud as he in turn supported us.

Of course, we didn't finish until 11.15pm. Which was interesting. Far too long, but we're working on that. In the subsequent two shows we've taken off six minutes a show just with a little judicious cutting and by simply speeding up. But we need to take off at least another 15 minutes. Which is possible and I'm sure we can do it.

But I loved playing Pistol and have really begun to find a progression through with him. I'm growing very fond of him, the old bluffer.

We had an unexpected morning off this morning. It felt very good. Like a whole extra day. Yesterday quite a few of us piled round to Clive Wood's and had a lovely roast lamb. He's the only one not utterly exhausted as *Henry V* is his play off, so he did the cooking. He's had his knackering bit, and in a week or so's time he'll be hard back at it, so he's enjoying it whilst it lasts.

Another long old notes session this afternoon, followed by working of scenes on stage. It's non-stop and even though I'm so darn tired I'm still loving it.

Like a kid with a toy.

WHAT a strange show we had last night. Coupled with it being a Monday evening (a Monday show after a tech week is always a strange show), and there being about 500 kids in, which always leads to an interesting evening, we had some technical problems too.

The biggest one was the disaster which happened to Anthony Bunsee on his trapeze. Halfway through the first half, it broke. With him on it. That is not a good thing to happen. Imagine swinging around on a trapeze and it suddenly breaking underneath you. Thank God he was only seven feet above the stage. What's more, everyone is clipped on to a secondary safety harness and he was lowered in gently to the floor on his separate automated line. All his training must have kicked in because he actually didn't need that second line: he clung desperately to the rope of the trapeze, and even tried carrying on with his speech – which I thought was above and beyond the call of duty.

My heart goes out to him. The 'French' have worked so hard – training for three hours a day for the last two months – to do their trapeze work for this show. And for a trapeze to break, well, that's just awful. Needless to say the problem has been addressed and all have been reassured that it will never happen again. Extra safety measures have been put in place alongside the already stringent procedures we have, so all our nerves, let alone the people that have to fly in this show, are settled.

It was just one of those shows. Tom Hodgkins fell down a trap. Just disappeared like Indiana Jones in a forest. Jon Slinger, instead of kicking me in the shin in the Fluellen/Pistol fight caught me in the knee. I went down like a sack of spuds. I'm hobbling about today but it'll be fine. Believe you me, when you're cramped up in pain from someone kicking you very hard in the knee and then you're having a leek forced down your mouth, it's no fun.

But it'll be fine tonight and we'll get back on track... And let's fly.

I T all starts with cards. On Monday morning I went and bought some nice lovely cards of some really beautiful images from the National Geographic.

Then, in the afternoon when I had a break from rehearsals on stage, I sat down in my dressing room and wrote to the 40-odd people I'm working with. Depending on how you're feeling this can either be a fearful chore or quite an exhilarating exercise. Luckily, I really got into it and came over all gushing to all my fellow actors, stage crew, designers, musicians, director – anyone within sight. It lasted for all the 45 or so cards. Kind of started putting me in the mood.

Next thing was, on the Tuesday, to check my brother knew it was a 7.00pm show (always the sign that something is up), and then it was a brief notes session early afternoon and suddenly other cards started appearing on my dressing room table as if delivered by some strange Hedwig of the theatre. Flowers bloom at Stage Door. Bottles of bubbly pop up in strange places. The air starts to fill with a weird tension and excitement that I can only describe as a frisson. Eyes brighten. Senses rule.

Yes, it's Press Night. The nearest theatre gets to Glamour.

As curtain up approaches people read their cards, do final warm ups, in my case – make small involuntary noises, take some air. Then 'Beginners' is announced – the Call to the Stage of those actors who start the play – and the hair goes up on the back of your neck. More noises. Everyone congregates in the Wings to watch Forbes as the Chorus do his Prologue and we're off, slapping him on the back as he comes offstage puffing his cheeks...

The show goes by in a whirl. I really enjoy it. Which is unusual for a Press Night. The only other time I've enjoyed Press Nights are in this project where we do

Press Days. Then you couldn't give a monkeys. It's too early and you've got three plays to do. And by the time you're on Play Three you've forgotten the Press are in at all. But it was great. We all gave a good account of ourselves. Geoffrey really flew. And we mucked up the Curtain Call. Which is always, in this company, a good sign.

We then had big party in the Foyer. My brother was there with my sister-in-law. They've got little Sam at 4 weeks old, so it was the first time they'd been up past half past nine for a month. We kept them awake, which is a bonus.

Then to a ceilidh, or however it's spelt. And now my head hurts. Another show tonight, and I'm sure it's going to rock. But we don't get cards or glamour for this one. Just headache pills and another dose of adrenalin. Which is far better.

WHAT is the meaning of the word 'play'? In this project we have been given access to a full exploration of this word in the context of the way humans interact and also of the 'Play' which we share with our audience.

10 November 2007

Even on Press Night of *Henry V*, such is the bond we have together now, we were able really to enjoy ourselves. I came off stage every time as Pistol knowing that I'd really loved being on there. Not showing off, but sharing the fun with everyone on stage and everyone watching. It is a unique feeling. And now, as we pitch straight back into the *Henry IV* technical rehearsals, we are rediscovering the sense of play in these plays too.

It's a tough schedule. Poor old Geoffrey. Having done the Press Night on Tuesday and had all the rollercoaster feelings of nerves, elation and exhaustion that 'Pressing' a play involves, he was in at midday the following day rehearsing with David Warner and Richard Cordery on Act 1 of *Henry IV Part I*. Then it was a show of *Henry V* in the evening, then at 10 o'clock the next day straight into Technical Rehearsals for *Part I*. By 7pm that evening we had started *Part II* which we forced through till midday the next day. Then it was a dress of *Part I*, then a performance of it in the evening. This morning we finished off teching *Part II* and now we have a dress this afternoon and performance of it tonight.

Phew.

Now, I'm not in *Part I* so, joy of joys, I had the evening off. I went round to a mate's place for some dinner and I was asleep on the sofa by 9 o'clock. But I asked the others how it went last night and to a person everyone said how much they'd ENJOYED it. How it was such fun to go back and not just rediscover but completely DISCOVER new things. How all on stage were playing.

The pressure from a very long summer was off and the Plays could begin to breathe. The audience seemed to love it. And so we're all really looking forward to tonight for the same again with *Part II*. Of all the eight plays we're doing in this History Cycle these two, *Henry IV Parts I & II*, will have to be the ones that will grow and mature and blossom most. They're so different from the other plays and yet all the passion, intensity and commitment that we bring to the others are all there. It's just that we are now beginning to find where it goes and place it properly.

As the days and milestones go by, we become tighter and tighter as a group. I cannot bear to think of this job finishing. We have a long way – and a lot of hard work – in front of us, but we all will cherish this forever.

And I'm sure, when this 'job' finishes, we will all start playing afresh having made friends for life.

YESTERDAY, Monday, we had technical rehearsals for *Richard II*. No rest for the wicked.

13 November 2007

A Sunday off after a big week and straight back at it. Anyway, we fair whipped through it and we got it finished at 5 o'clock which meant that for the first time in a long time we had the evening off as a company. We all piled to the pub naturally, and after three very nice pints I decided to give my liver a rest, get on my bike and head home. The thought of cooking something, sitting down and watching some telly for the first time in ages was too much.

It was bloody freezing and off I sped, powering up the hill, and as I turned in to my driveway in the dark, I was hit full on the broadside by a badger.

I let out interesting involuntary noises again. So much so that my flatmate Josefa, high up in the top of the house, wondered if I was calling to her. The beast had got me! Straight from the starboard side and hit me amidships. Claws. Teeth. A blur of black and white. It torpedoed underneath my pedal and got my left boot. There's a tooth mark on it.

Somehow, I managed to stay on the bike and carry on. I ventured a panicked look round. There was the creature, slightly dazed, in a heap, eyeing me with what can only be described as malevolence, while I stared back in a mixture of defiance and underwear-moistening fear. Those things are big when you're going eyeball to eyeball with them. Vicious.

I parked my bike. Sod the lock, I thought, I'm about to get throated by a manic badger. And I shot upstairs with alarming speed. Breathless, I regaled my story to a frankly unimpressed Josefa, and for medicinal purposes only, had to tuck into a bottle of red that happened to be left over from the cast party we'd had at mine on Sunday. Out went the telly and the cooking et al and thus, yet again, I woke up this morning with a headache. And a tooth mark on my boot.

So if getting attacked by demented badgers is what happens in Stratford on a night off then roll on the Octology! Tonight we do *Richard II* for the first time in three months and we had a good Dress of it this afternoon. It's such an enjoyable show to do. I found myself once again almost sighing out loud at the beauty of some of the language.

But not as loud as when the beast badger got me. Now THAT was interesting language...

19 November 2007

W E'RE deep into understudy rehearsals for *Richard II* now.

As I write it's lunchtime on Monday and we've a run through this afternoon, a technical tomorrow then the actual run on Wednesday afternoon. Then I start getting my life back.

It's been so hard the last two weeks, first Pressing *Henry V* and then straight into re-mounting the *Henry IVs* whilst understudy rehearsing *Richard II* by day. Dodging badgers.

I didn't write last week for fear that I might've been sued for slander to anyone and everyone. I was knackered, feeling ill and severely cheesed off with everyone who is not in *Richard II* for having three days off last week then another three this week whilst we've been working without a day off for the last eight weeks...

But I told myself to grow up, get a life and get on with it. Life's too short and I've had worse. It ain't anybody's fault and that's the way the cookie crumbles.

Which is all true, but doesn't stop me being knackered. Although after a brilliantly wet Sunday (the badgers don't come out), I feel revived and refreshed even though I spent half the day learning lines. My time for a little rest will be after Wednesday where I will only be performing in the evenings whilst the others do understudy rehearsals for the *Henry IVs* by day, so it all pans out. This will be the first time, twenty-one months in, that I will just be performing in the evenings in this entire job.

I won't know what to do with myself.

S LEEP. I have begun to reacquaint myself with it over the last four or five days. And readers, isn't it just great? Jeez, I'd forgotten how nice it is. 27 November 2007

I haven't written in a while because we were so busy up until Wednesday of last week and then I had a whole day off and after that, frankly, I just couldn't be bothered. We did a lovely *Part II* on Friday night and then a nice little couple of *Henry Vs* on Saturday. This is the part of the project where I can sit back and really let go. The simple act of playing in a costume every night. Shouting in the evenings (as Patrick Troughton once said about acting).

I'm beginning to love playing Pistol even more. And Bushy in *Richard II* is such a weirdo that I'm just beginning to rather enjoy him too. Michael gave me a note about him the other day which basically said just to enjoy and celebrate the beauty and impenetrability of the words Our Man Will gives Bushy. In other words, nobody's going to understand a word I say but if I say it nicely people like it anyway. Which is fine by me. Story of my life.

Having time off, after being so busy, takes a bit of a while getting used to. It was only two days – Sunday and Monday – but it felt like three weeks. I even had a meeting yesterday (Monday) on my day off for the Artists' Forum which the RSC runs. This is a representative forum where actors can give feedback and voice questions or concerns to management, and they in turn can supply information, ask questions and debate with the actors. I turned up grumpy from the start but inwardly, I was very happy. I think what made me grumpy was the whitewashed sterilisation of a once lovely building that was the Union Club on Chapel Lane.

From the outside they have achieved the unique feat of turning it from a nice-looking late Georgian building into something resembling a cross between a disused mental home and a business park. The room in which we sat could have been in any room in any office in Anytown, Dumbandblandshire.

The RSC, to my mind, is the greatest theatre company in the world and certainly the best THEATRE company I've ever worked for. Their support, welfare systems, practice and brief are the best I have ever known and it is a community and family I will always cherish. We have to remember also that all the actors, directors, designers, stage crew, wardrobe, wigs, everyone, we are all rogues and vagabonds. I know I am. We don't live normally. I made a decision when I was sixteen that I was never going to work in some branded corporate office. I was hopefully going to create something and I was going to live that life. Be silly. Be joyful. And the RSC has been a prime contributor to me being able to do that. We should never be bland.

I said as much in the meeting and then, of course, felt very tired because it was my day off. So I went to the pub and had a glass of wine – just because I could. Went home and fell asleep, dribbling, on the sofa. Sleep again. Perchance to dream.

Now that, my friends, is a DAY OFF.

WE did *Richard II* on Tuesday night. As per, I enjoyed it again more and more.

29 November 2007

Bushy becomes ever more camp. However, in Act 4 scene 1 – the scene where Richard gives the crown to Bolingbroke, which is preceded by the challenging of the nobles: all of them throwing gloves at each other willy-nilly, I'm playing the Abbot of Westminster, standing up on the first balcony on the tower looking Vulcan, when Lex Shrapnel managed to do one of the funniest things I've seen on stage for a long time. There he was, all Hotspur and butch, giving it large in leather and he challenges the Lord Aumerle (Jimmy Tucker) with his glove. He lifts his arm high to throw it manfully at him, and at its very apogee, the glove sails from his hand. His arm continues to throw the thing but it isn't there. It's sailing like a feather down on to the stage far behind him.

Dumbfounded, he turns like a trained dancer, fetches it, and realising that all manly cover is blown, throws it rather artfully in the vague direction of said Aumerle/Jimmy who did very well I thought to restrain himself.

I, on the other hand, didn't. I let out a loud guffaw and was openly laughing on stage. Now, dear reader, it may not seem that funny. But corpsing – the dark world of bursting into laughter on stage – can come from the smallest of things. Let me say here that no actor will actively condone corpsing – let alone in this company. Let's face it, if you've paid good money to come and see a play, the last thing you want is some half-arsed actor giggling his way through the lines. But it happens. It's theatre. It's live. We are real humans up there. And sometimes you just can't help yourself. You try, man, you try.

I fell this time into the classic corpsing mode. I laughed openly then spent the next half minute or so resembling a man in the latter stages of constipation, my face contorting to a rictus grin. I pulled myself together. I was fine. What was I fine from? Thus the image of Lex and his glove returns like a ticking bomb. Your stomach leaps. The muscles go and you silently guffaw again. Tears appeared in my eyes. These I thought I could turn to my advantage, as I tried artfully to turn my shame into portraying the emotion the Abbot was feeling at the unfolding scene. Letting the tears flow – my face a portrait of angst. Honest. I'm sure I just looked like a bloke trying not to laugh. Like a guilty schoolboy before a master.

Then you think you've cracked it. The tightness goes. You're back. You're in the scene. All is good. But then, out of nowhere, the image comes zinging into

your brain like an eagle to its prey. More tears. More
constipation. 'Actoplasm' all over the stage. Thank
God I didn't have to speak until the end of the scene. It
wouldn't've been pretty. Or intelligible, for that matter.

The scene ends. The horror ends. Others come off stage
bearing similar signs of tears and pain. Lex couldn't
speak. The exhaled wheezes and screams of laughter let
out filled the air round the back of the Courtyard.

The spirit of Ensemble lives on...

O N Monday I went back to school.

5 December 2007

It's always an unnerving experience, as
whenever I go into a school I always smell the
unmistakable whiff of overcooked stale vegetables
whether it's there or not. It wasn't this time, and what
greeted me were two fantastic pieces of theatre. I'd
been asked by Sarah Talbot, the new Head of Drama at
King Edward's School – the school Shakespeare went
to and just round the back of The Courtyard Theatre
itself – to see two pieces. One was by the Year 10 boys
of her school and the other was by the Year 10 girls of
their sister school the Shottery School for Girls. They
had been to see our production and these were two
short pieces in response to *Henry V*.

Well, they were fantastic. Absolutely brilliant.
The girls went first and produced a beautiful female
response to war, with images of death and destruction,
creeping murmur and loss played out with their
collective shapes all just on the school gym floor. At

the end, each performer had given one end of a red ribbon to one central girl standing on a chair, hands out Christ-on-a-cross-like, whilst the other end stretched, Maypole-like, to their bodies lying dead upon the ground. Beautiful and really effective at the same time.

The boys then produced a classic male response to war, with some fantastic fighting. As Fight Captain in The Histories Company, I can honestly say there were some brilliant and faintly alarming bits of stage fighting there. But there was exceptional storytelling here too, and their responses at the end as all died on the stage whilst calling names of famous battles through the ages was very moving.

What was so great to me as an actor trying every night to communicate words to an audience was how well they obviously understood the lines and the whole play. It was a real joy and a gratification to see. These guys knew what they were doing. And they understood the power of language – what it is they are actually saying. I said as much afterwards when I said a few words and got them to clap each other again. They deserved it. A few beaming parents were there, and for some reason, I felt as proud as they were.

It was our night off that night so the whole experience deserved a couple or three in the Duck, I thought, by way of celebration. Even both Heads of Drama from the schools came and had a small glass. I take my hat off to them. Or rather, raise my glass. I couldn't do what they do, day in day out. Their commitment and joy to their subject and the kids they teach is so strong. And they're obviously good at their job. They are brilliant. And the smell of stale vegetables in school has been banished forever from my mind.

Phew.

I WAS sitting in the bath this morning when I noticed something strange.

8 December 2007

This, sadly, is not a regular occurrence. I even mentioned it to Lex Shrapnel during the show this afternoon and he looked at me askance and said quietly that he had it too.

Yes, dear reader, you guessed it. We have the beginnings of calluses on our knees. I've just asked one of the French and they have them on their hands. Sigh.

Now an STD – Strenuous Theatrical Disorder – is not too much to worry about, but really, we all spend so much time crawling around on our hands and knees under the stage in *Henry V* that we're actually beginning to grow things. I can't believe it!

Couple that with an unfortunate tear in my trousers this afternoon and I had a cracking show. I first ripped them as I went down the small trap backstage that is the access to substage. I had no time to go to wardrobe, flapping, so I went on and did the 'once more unto the breech, dear friends, once more…' scene. Then there was the silent creep out of the traps (more crawling) and on to the scene where Pistol pleads for Fluellen to save Bardolph's life.

During the scene we react lots of times to the bangs and explosions of the battle by ducking under the stage. Each time I ducked, so the tear in my trousers increased. By the time the scene ended I was faintly surprised that they were on at all. It was mighty windy. Which, again, is nothing unusual, but this time I knew it wasn't me. Still, Wardrobe had a good go at them in the interval and all was mended by the second half.

But I think I shall have to get them to sew some kneepads into the trousers. It may make Pistol look like an American Football player, but at least I'll be able to take a bath without worrying.

I WAS sat sprawled across Clive Wood's sofa yesterday (Sunday – bliss), glass of wine in hand, a bellyful of chicken successfully negotiated, when I looked across at Rob Carroll, similarly plastered over a chair, and remembered that Rob was Clive's understudy.

I suppose it is a big indication of the way we are all working together and for each other that it hadn't even occurred to me, whilst it was going on, to write that we had a major understudy situation two weeks ago.

Clive, due to a big family illness, had to miss the show on Tuesday two weeks ago and Rob had to go on as Bolingbroke in *Richard II*. Believe you me, that is a big ask. Well, he was brilliant. Cool and calm as you like, just went out and delivered. Bang. Just like that. There's life in the hairy Australian yet. And then he had to go on the next night and play the title role in *Henry IV Part I*.

It was a real example of how the support we have for each other can go such a long way. He was in great company and we were all right behind him and off he flew. It was very exciting to watch.

We also had a situation the previous week where Luke Neal, having been sick all day, went on to do the show that night, *Henry V*, where he plays the Duke of Gloucester. Halfway through Act 1 sc 2 he quietly walked off stage and vomited into a bucket. The most impressive thing was that he managed to do it quietly.

I was standing there as Pistol and it was an edifying
sight just before I went on. Stage Management sent him
home. Which meant, of course, that we had to change
on the hoof. Chris McGill, seeing he was off, quick as
a flash took Luke's lines and for the rest of the play we
were all running around, taking Luke's lines and doing
all the stuff he does in the play with trap doors and the
like. Took it in our stride.

Due to the nature of this project, understudy rehearsals
are a nightmare to fit in. We rehearsed the *Richard II*
understudy stuff underneath the principal rehearsals
for *Henry IV Part II* back in May. This meant I learnt
my understudy lines back in April having gone through
them in rehearsal only once since then until now. You
have to be on your toes. Then, when we were rehearsing
Henry V in London, we rehearsed the understudies for
Henry IV *Parts I & II*, as well as the *Henry V* understudy
stuff. All very confusing and complicated.

Having mounted and opened *Henry V*, not content
with playing four different shows by night we are now
in understudy rehearsals on stage for all those four
shows by day.

We are reaching the end, as I've just come out of a
fight call for the Pistol/Fluellen understudy fight. The
final understudy run of this project will be on Thursday.
On Friday we do a special scene for the RSC's Annual
General Meeting, then after two shows Saturday we
are going to have the mother of all parties. It will be
messy. It will be cruel. But, boy, it will be good. Slinger,
Costain and McGill are DJ'ing. Wahey!

Now, in the middle of all that Rob had to go on
and produce the goods to a paying audience. He was
prepared and he was brilliant. We were all there for him
and he said that he felt really good.

Understudying is the hardest job in acting. You have to go on and do a performance with about 2% of the rehearsal time the principal gets. The lines are seemingly just at the end of your grasp and you're acting with people that you've never done the scene with. It's tough, but can be the biggest thrill of all.

And as Rob sat slumped across the chair at Clive's yesterday, with Clive's family all back to health, I know that he sits there with just a little bit more experience under his belt, maybe a small grey hair in his head, but with the smile of a job well done.

Now that's a Sunday.

21 December 2007

WHAT a weird and wonderful week it was. I haven't written because we were so busy and then, alleluia, we had Sunday, Monday and Tuesday off. I got my Christmas tree up and some tinsel round the window and everything. It's been strange coming back this week to do the shows, and I've really liked doing them as a consequence.

But, most importantly, we had the understudy run of *Henry V* on Thursday last week. It was superb. All the performances were so strong, all were working for each other. Chris McGill deserves a medal for doing Hal in both the *Henry IV*s and *Henry V* – that is a fearful amount of lines and entrances and exits and fights and moves and thoughts and emotions – with such a small amount of rehearsal time.

I think it is such an indicator of the strength of this ensemble that he and we pulled all that off. And a lesson for future ensembles that we must need more

time to fit all that in. It is not something that the paying
public have to know about, but it is a necessary and
vital part of our practice. And it's bloody knackering.
The sheer number of hours that we spend in this
building – the dear young Courtyard. And they must
needs sort out the drains too…

We then did our bit for the Company by doing an
extract from *Henry V* the next day for the AGM and
Prince Charles. He came and met us afterwards, and
then he stayed and saw the show, so he obviously liked
the brief trailer in the afternoon. He popped backstage
and had a word with a few of us after the show again.
He seemed to really like it and I apologised for smelling
of leek. Which is not something you do every day to the
heir to the throne.

Doing *Henry V* knowing he was in the audience was
interesting, because after all we're doing a play about
his family. There are some pretty edgy lines about the
nature of kingship in that play and they had a little extra
zing to them that night. Still, it was a great show as
we'd not been working our guts out during the day and
felt let off the leash and the audience seemed to love it,
which is much more important.

This is our one free week of just performing, then
it's Christmas! We get four days off, which is a pretty
much unheard-of luxury for any actor working over
Christmas. We don't do a show till the 28th! Mind you,
we do a Trilogy Day on the 29th so that should work off
the Christmas dinner…

Then we have New Year's Eve off! My, ambassador,
you are really spoiling us. Still, we are doing *Richard II*
on New Year's Day which should be an intriguing little
number. I wouldn't sit in the front row if I were you.
Then, dear friends, the *coup de grâce*; the icing on the
cake; the *pièce de résistance*: yes, we start re-rehearsals

on January 2nd for *Henry VI*, yes Henry the 6th, *Part I*.
Blimey O'Reilly.

This is going to be a major shock to the system.
A week later we have, on consecutive days, a walking
UNDERSTUDY line run of *Henry VI Parts I & II*! This is
cruel. Bang goes my holiday. I'm going to be spending it
poring over lines for the *Henry VIs*. Sigh.

Never mind – I'm still having the time of my life. It's
been a fantastic year. And next year is when the whole
of this enormous project comes together and we'll be
doing all eight shows. It is very very exciting. Especially
with all the tinsel round me window.

I hope that all of you have a wonderful Christmas
and New Year. Have a good one. Badgers permitting,
we will.

3 January 2008

WELL, a very Happy New Year to everyone!

The ritual is over for another year. All the
magic; the things we do the same every year; the
wonder of presents, reindeers, colours and the hope
of snow. The party, the drink and the Auld Lang Syne.
I hope you had a lovely time. Something very special
took place here too, and it is not unconnected.

We were all standing in the tunnel behind the big
double doors just before we started *Richard II* on the
28th December. We call it the 'Hell Mouth'. It's called
this because when Michael first had the concept for the
staging of these plays he took the view that the *Henry
VIs* and *Richard III* were the 'last great medieval plays'

and acted as a conduit through which Shakespeare
began to form his/our view of modernity in theatre. You
could say the doors on stage represent those doors of
perception opening in Shakespeare's mind.

But they are definitely rooted in the medieval
Mystery and Morality Plays (and indeed Mummers
Plays), which took place for a few hundred years before,
where the entrance to the stage was usually conceived
as the entrance for the characters in the play to or from
Heaven or Hell.

The Plays would have a Keeper, not only to guard the
gates but to let people in who had learnt their salvation,
and would comment and be alive in the action on stage.
Thus we have The Keeper in our productions who
ushers out characters that may even come back again,
having learnt some lessons, to influence what comes
later in the story. Hence our reference to it as 'The
Hell Mouth'. These plays themselves are rooted in the
passage of time from our very first beginnings. They
touch something as we watch.

It was our first show back after an unprecedented four
nights off over Christmas. Everyone was touched with
a little bit of ye olde Xmas cheer and there was more
guffawing, giggling and gaffes than usual behind those
doors as we waited for Rob to do the mobile phone
announcement out front. Others stand still, preparing
Others quietly warm up their mouths and voices.
Others crack jokes. There we all are in the dark, we've
been there a thousand times. Rob takes his place, noting
that he missed his vocation as a stand-up, as we can
hear the audience settle down in anticipation. Guffaw,
wheeze, giggle, fart, noise, tut, giggle, cough. Then the
doors open. And something truly mystical happens.

We are as one. We move as one. We do the whole
slow dance (or 'blob' as we call it) utterly in sync,

harmony, whatever you want to call it. Something has happened to us which makes us totally together. The audience are sucked in and we are utterly absorbed.

And then we're off. Bang, the whole show goes by. And even though we put a few minutes on the show, it's electric. This feeds into *Henry IV Part I* the next day, where a lot of the audience had seen the show the previous evening, and again into *Part II*. *Henry V* that night is on fire. When we finish, the reception is extraordinary. We even brought the house lights back up but they refused to stop clapping and we went back on. It was very special. Our own ritual – like Christmas Day every night – was truly done.

What is it that makes this so mystical? Theatre, like Christmas, like New Year, like marriages, funerals, christenings, like Halloween, is a ritual. All Western theatre comes originally from the essence of ritual when, in our ancestral villages, we danced and sang to reaffirm and celebrate our existence and ward off any nasties and thoughts that may be out there. To tell and sing stories is to affirm that we are. That we exist. Scholars have come up with three central tenets, the hangers, if you like, upon which most human ritual was based and which carry on into our modern rituals today. These are Separation, Liminality and Aggregation.

The first, Separation, is when the protagonists of the ritual are separated from the rest of the group. For example, in our modern marriage ceremony, the bride and groom are traditionally separated from each other the night before their wedding, and also the families and friends all congregate – with both families separated – before the bride arrives. So too at the theatre. We, the actors, are separated from the audience half an hour before the performance/ritual starts. Any visitors are hoofed out the building. And audiences

themselves get a bit twitchy if they see an actor they're
about to view pottering by licking an ice cream ten
minutes before they go on.

The second, Liminality, is the act of crossing.
The threshold point. Something happens where the
protagonist literally crosses over from one point to the
next. They cross the *limen* – the fine texture between
one thing and another. In marriages today this is
represented by the bride stepping through the door,
the congregation rising, and her 'walking down the
aisle' between the two families. The lifting of the veil.
The kissing of the bride. It is deep within us. Again it
is represented by the groom picking up his bride and
literally carrying her over the threshold. He carries her
from one state to another. In the theatre, the lights go
down, the drum rolls, the curtains rise, the hairs on the
back of any audience's neck rise with it. In our case, the
doors open and we step on stage. We are in that liminal
point. A state rooted in the origins of ritual. Of our
society itself.

The third state, Aggregation, is the academic word
for a bloody great party. Again, if you take marriage
today, it wouldn't seem right without a big wingding
after it. So too with our ancestors. And in the theatre,
so the audience clap as one to recognise what has just
happened. There is the hum of what the audience have
just witnessed. And in our case, it is the brief walk to
the Duck and the few drinks inside to celebrate. The
audience are there. So are we. And the show is there too
somehow.

This for me is as much a ritual as dancing around the
fire or whatever it was our ancestors did back then. We
stood in the Hell Mouth and we crossed the limen. The
doors open and something happens to us. That mystical
ancient process by which we can perform.

And as we stand now at the threshold of one year into another I can really feel those doors opening. As I write, we are just about to start a walking line run of *Henry VI Part I*. A play I first rehearsed in 2000 when I was 29. And we last performed 11 months ago. We, as an ensemble, are standing on the threshold of something truly great. No other group of actors has ever staged these eight History Plays in their entirety in such a concentrated period of time. We are very lucky. We are making history whilst portraying History.

And it is in that playing; in that ritual; in that repetition; that affirmation; that Christmas-like appeal to our senses every night, that we, and hopefully our audiences, find our Magic.

Happy New Year!

16 January 2008

HOLIDAYS? What holidays?!
We are engaged in performing four shows by night and restaging four different shows by day. And restaging all the understudy work as well. This is a lot of work. And my mind has turned to slush.

Since our week off, we did *Henry VI Part III* for the first time in 11 months on Monday morning. In the afternoon we did an understudy run of *Henry VI Part I*. In the evening we performed *Henry V*. On Tuesday morning we did an understudy run of *Henry VI Part II*. In the afternoon, a run of *Richard III*. We performed *Henry V* again. This morning we did a full, principal run of *Henry VI Part I*. And this afternoon we have a line run of *Richard II* and then a performance of the same play this evening. Tomorrow we rehearse all the fights in the *Henry VIs* – there are 33 broadsword fights on those shows – and perform in the evening.

This, dear readers, is utter madness. Some people have taken to shouting: 'EXTREME HISTORY!!!' like we're on some absurd Channel Four documentary or something.

It is extraordinary how the body acts before the conscious brain. Muscle memory kicks in and you find yourself doing and saying things on stage that I had no actual memory of before. Your body just goes stage left there, and then stage right over there, upstage here and downstage there; something opens my mouth and makes the right words come out at roughly the right time. It is an out-of-body, or rather out-of-mind experience.

Mind you, we've had a few glitches in the matrix. I was saying 'Nay...' to something as my character, the Duke of Somerset, in *Henry VI Part II* and suddenly my mind slipped on to the Pistol motorway in my brain and off I went, saying, 'Nay, rather damn them with King Cerberus and let the welkin roar!' which is from *Henry IV Part II*. Interesting.

Geoffrey Streatfeild was warming up for *Henry V* at half past six last night and had a little mental blank and had to go to the props cupboard behind the audience to establish which play it was we were doing. I think he was faintly surprised and alarmed to find it was *Henry V*.

Jon Slinger was in the middle of a *Richard III* speech yesterday and launched seamlessly into *Richard II* for a line before returning, ashen-faced, back to *Richard III*.

It's all very exciting. And also very knackering. And we will not stop for breath now until this mad, crazy, wonderful project ends. Still, the holidays were nice.

'YOU stink,' said Keith Bartlett to me in the Hell Mouth backstage during the run through of *Henry VI Part II* on Wednesday, 'Your pits are howling.' Which is nice, isn't it?

But, frankly, they were. I was humming. Due to waking up late and haring out the door with ne'er so much as a look at the bathroom, cycling like a banshee into work and making it into the theatre with about five seconds to spare; and then an unscheduled and fragrant game of table tennis in the interval, by the time Jack Cade came along in the second half and Keith was passing by my raised aloft arms, I was ready to stop people at a hundred yards.

Which isn't very ensemble of me, is it? Now, I've known Keith for nearly eight years and if he can't drop me a hint and tell me to go and have a shower then nobody can. Honesty, when you're working physically so close to each other for 13 or so hours every day, is by far the best policy.

As it also is with our rehearsal schedule. And as Michael Boyd has been with our workload. These are tough times for us at the moment. The sheer physical effort of rehearsing all day and then trying to perform to our best at night is nearly breaking us.

As a consequence, the company nearly revolted on Tuesday when faced with a punishing rehearsal too far. The good thing is that people listened and whilst everyone was still a bit tetchy for a day or two, it weirdly made the run of *Henry VI Part II* in the afternoon a cheeky little affair. I was squaring up to Clive in the Petitioner's scene and he punched me in the chest; now, he is my best mate so if you're going to punch someone it might as well be your best mate, in my book. (Mind you, he was probably trying to fend off the smell, I don't know.)

There was some genuine emotion going on out there. But we all got in on Friday and the mood had significantly changed. We did the whole of *Henry VI Part III* in the morning, and notes and rehearsals in the afternoon, and not a sausage was there about anything. We were all laughing and giggling again. We had got something out of our system.

Whilst the collective noun for actors should be a 'whinge', we in this company, I think, have been generally pretty good over the last two years. And we weren't complaining for nothing. Rehearsals should have a proper direction to them at this stage, and if they don't then we are better off resting. And there's no point faffing about on stage if we're all there with a bucket-load of resentment. Nothing will get done. But Michael listened and things have changed.

As happened with my armpits. Which is better for everyone concerned.

■

4 February 2008

LAST Friday we were rehearsing *Henry VI Part II* Act 3 Scene 1.

Michael was talking to us about it, giving us his notes, and after a while, Richard Cordery, one of the prime movers in the scene, burst out with 'I'm so sorry!'.

I thought he might've farted or something, but no: 'I'm completely in the wrong scene. I thought it was *Henry VI Part ONE* Act 3 sc 1 we were doing, not *Part TWO*. I've been standing here wondering what on earth you were talking about for five minutes.'

A few minutes later Tom Hodgkins makes a point about the scene only to be greeted with blank stares and a communal question: 'Are you talking about the same scene as us?' 'Yeah, 'course I am,' replies Tom. A minute or two later as we gather to do the scene, Tom says, 'Wait a minute, what are you lot doing? Isn't this Act 1 sc 3 *Part II*?'. 'NO!!' I cry, 'it's Act 3 sc 1 *Part II*!'

As you can see, things are getting confusing. We had to do *Henry IV Part I* that night. It's a small miracle we even got on to do the first scene. It was my night off and I only realised at the fight call that I wasn't needed and was gently told to go home and get some sleep.

And, as I write, it's lunchtime on Monday and I've spent two hours hanging upside down from a ladder covered in blood. Yes, it's *Henry VI Part I* time again and we are in technicals for it. I love this show! And, including the time we did it in 2000/1 this is my sixth tech for it. Sigh. For me, this show is a belter. I'm running around like a blue-arsed fly all the time and the only time I get to have a rest is when I'm on stage…

But it's crazy times. I first 'teched' these plays when I was 29. Next week on Wednesday, I turn 37 and we'll be teching *Henry VI Part III*. A fact I'm faintly horrified and also absurdly proud about too. We were teching *Richard III* on my 30th birthday. The day after my 37th I will start teching it again. Strange and heady times. There's a great Czech film made in the seventies called *Tomorrow, I Will Wake Up and Scald Myself With Tea*. That pretty much sums it up. The difference of course is that I AM seven years older. A little wiser. A little older. A little stronger. Hopefully, a better actor.

Mind you, with all these different scenes and acts and plays and fights, I've got the impression that dementia is setting in somewhat early. Just ask Richard Cordery…

TECHING *Part III* this morning and flush from
the Poker Tournament yesterday, Miss Alexia
'Cincinnati' Healy is triumphant.

So she should be. Anthony Holden, who was there,
has written books not only on Shakespeare but on Poker
too, so when he heard that we, as an ensemble, were
having a poker tournament he was up here like a rat up
a drainpipe.

Strangely, he didn't win; he came second. Some
geezer called Carl from Stratford won. But 'Cincinnati'
came third which is a considerable achievement
considering she only played the game for the first time
three weeks ago. I lost everything in the first hour and
was up moodily stomping around the hills watching the
sunset as Alexia was holding 'em and folding 'em. Hats
off to Keith Bartlett for organising it (what was it I said
about him being a seven year-old boy with a fifty year-
old face…?) and running it so smoothly.

Which also can be said of our technical rehearsals
for the remounting of all these *Henry VIs*. The stage
management and crew have all been fantastic, as have
all the new dressers that have come in or returned.
Everyone is working so hard. And doing *Henry VI Part
I & II* last week was a real joy for me. The lines are part
of me now. Even though I don't say that much in *Part II*,
I'm on all the time and it was electric to be back doing
it all again. To see it all being informed by what we have
done in the intervening year, it now feels like we are
beginning to complete the jigsaw.

There is a pitch to how much we can produce at any
one time however. We seem to have developed a weird
instinct as to how much we can give collectively in a

dress and technical so that it is the performance that gets our full energy. It's not spoken or judged, just felt and done. This is the benefit of working so closely together for the last two years. And also a result of being so tired that we've stopped bothering to think and just done it instead. Which, in my case, is always a good thing. The moment I start using my brain before I perform is always a cause for alarm in my book. It always gets in the way.

Which is why I'm useless at Poker and Alexia wins...

12 February 2008

REHEARSING fights this morning, Juliette, one of our Stage Management, brought in a set of scales and had to weigh everyone who enters on the metal bridge which gets flown in at various intervals throughout these eight shows, just in case there's been any massive weight changes which will put the bridge out of kilter.

The cheek! This made Michael start musing about how an opportunity was missed on measuring the differences in us from the start to the end of the project. Our weight, our right arms from lifting a sword and rope climbing, our legs from the weight of all those costumes, our hippocampus which carries the weight of all our words we keep in our heads.

Our sense of time would be an interesting measurement too. One of the fights to rehearse was the Somerset/Richard fight in *Henry VI Part II*. It's always been a problem because we've wanted to tell a clear story with it in the sense that the fight shifts so that

Somerset ends up appearing to win, and then through Richard's cunning – i.e. grabbing Somerset's dagger which is in a holster on his breastplate and stabbing Somerset with it – he wins the fight and kills Somerset in a really nasty, horrible way.

We've shifted it around a bit now and made sure that the knife can really be seen by the audience. I still get to cough and spit blood all over Jon's face, so it remains very gratifying. So a fight which Jon and I rehearsed first in April 2006 is still changing, living, breathing and refined. Time is not an obstacle and we should never let ourselves become jaded with its passage.

One of the many very strange things about this extraordinary job is the way time shifts. It's not like any other job. For most actors, to be told you were doing a four month job with many performances in Stratford and then transferring to London into The Roundhouse for two months, which is what we are now faced with, they would bite your hand off in accepting it.

Such is the nature of this job, because it is so long, that the icy hand of unemployment and the search for work has begun to finger our collar even though we still have a long and very hard-working way to go.

I spoke to my agent for the first time in a year and a half the other day. What happens next? How am I going to earn some money? Make a living? For so long, we have had the wonderful privilege of living and earning and working, and it feels strange to have to think about returning to that default position of the actor – the insecurity, the terror, the letter from the bank, the rejection. But also the joy, the acceptance, the chance to lead a different life, the chance to scream. The whole rollercoaster gamut of experience that is being an actor. For the first time I find myself thinking of it even

though we have a long, but comparatively short, way
to go.

And it fair makes me shrivel up inside.

But we have time. To quote Dylan Thomas: 'Listen.
Time passes.' And it's my birthday tomorrow so time
can pass away. Another year notched on the sickle
and another year to LOOK FORWARD TO! And who
knows, I might get a job after this. Stranger things have
happened. At least I could say that my hippocampus is
extremely large.

21 February 2008

B LEEEUURGHHH!!!!
That's what I felt I sounded like on stage last
night. Now, there are two things going on here.

The first, of course, is cabin fever and manifests
itself firstly with small involuntary noises made whilst
reading the script, say, in the Green Room. These noises
become part of you. Everyone makes them and they
become inaudible to you or to colleagues. Any outsider
listening in may raise an eyebrow but frankly, at this
stage, they can whistle.

Then, like an addiction, they grow insidiously. They
become sudden exclamations. Vocal twitches which
catch out not only the issuer but anybody within twenty
feet. The body starts to cramp and spasm. Arms fly
at weird angles. Teeth are sucked and spat out again,
cheeks billowing.

Then you run, mad and staring, through the back
stage area into a wall. You look at the clock on said wall
and it reads 10.45. It's only after a thorough mental
search you realise it's the morning and not the evening

and that you will still be here when the clock returns
to that position in twelve hours' time. Even a Histories
actor will tell the right time twice a day.

The second thing going on here, extreme mental
tiredness, involves brain spasms. Take yesterday. I
spent the first half of the morning finishing a technical
understudy rehearsal of *Henry VI Part I* where I play
the Duke of York AND the Bishop of Winchester. Then
for the rest of the morning and afternoon it was an
understudy tech rehearsal of *Henry VI Part II* – again
playing York and Winchester.

Then it was a performance of *Henry VI Part II* in the
evening, where I play the Duke of Somerset. In Act 1 sc
3, York and Somerset come storming on with the King,
and York says, 'If York hath ill demeaned himself in
France/ Let him be denayed the Regentship', to which
Somerset replies, 'If Somerset be unworthy of the place/
Let York be Regent, I will yield to him'.

On we came. Clive says his line as York. I open my
mouth and I speak utter pants. It's too much for me.
The whole – York/Somerset who the hell am I, hang
on, I've been putting in twelve hour days for weeks
now and I've forgotten my own name let alone my
character's or any other character I've ever played in my
life – thing kicked in. Nothing. Not a sausage.

But, wait a second sunshine, you say, I'm a
professional actor; these people looking at me have paid
good money to see you strutting your stuff, not some
pathetic simpleton who looks as though he's got lost
in an asylum. Get yourself together. You'll never work
again. Aaaargh! The world is turning black. Eh? What's
that noise?

It's someone speaking.

Slowly, achingly, I realise it's coming from
somewhere near me. In fact it IS me. I'm saying
something. It's my line. It's Somerset's line. I'm on stage.

I'm in the scene. I've finished the line. And other people
are responding. And I'm back! All that's taken place
in my head has taken about a third of a second. Long
enough for adrenalin to be surging around my body,
sweat beading on my head. The audience would never
know but it's enough for me to wet my pants.

'Drying' is a horrible experience and one no actor, a
species who will take the Mickey mercilessly out of
anything, will make light of. It can and has happened
to us all. We are so tired, so exhausted at the moment
that maybe because of this it happened to me last night.
It was infinitesimal but it really shocked me. I spoke a
bit of drivel for half a line, but it was fine. We're at that
pitch now.

    Michael Boyd has been quoted in the press as saying
he likes to drive his actors to the point of exhaustion,
and then you get something quite new and interesting
out of them. Point taken, but it's seat of the pants stuff.
Quite exciting, though.

There is certainly no danger of the brain getting in the
way. I read a fantastic quote from Peter Ustinov the
other day when he was faced with a particularly fervent
Method actor in the 1950s to whom he said: 'Don't just
do something. Stand there!' We are at that rather nice
point in performance where, in my view, we are faced
with no choice but just to be there. Be present.

    And that, to me, is the secret of acting. I don't know
whether it's the old adage of 'Get on stage, say the lines,
don't bang into the furniture, and get off stage', firstly
because we don't have any furniture, and secondly
because we care, but it is a useful note. Because the
plays will perform and we are in them. The swords
do the fighting. And we do the talking. It's as simple
as that.

Except, of course, when you're making noises and running into the wall and wondering who you are and where the Dickens you came from. Easy, really.

█

SITTING on the sofa at about 1.15am last night, thinking about trying to go to bed after a rip-roaring show, and not to HAVE to finish the last bit of wine in the glass, I felt – literally felt – a noise, and the hairs rose on my neck. It gathered in sound, the telly started to wobble on its crap little stand and a DVD fell off. Glasses clinked.

27 February 2008 (Morning)

I thought for a wild moment it might be one of the ghosts which are supposed to potter about this old house. But then, in an even wilder moment, I realised the whole house was shaking. A real, physical shaking. It grew and grew. I wasn't scared – I just had absolutely no idea what to do. I sat there, rumbling. The noise increased, then one of the old, old beams gave a squeak and a crack. I let out a 'Whoah!' and a fart, and then it stopped.

It stopped. What the...?

It must have been an earthquake, pure and simple. My flatmate, Josefa, came creeping from her room and put her head round the door: 'Did you just...?'

Having assured her it wasn't me, she sat utterly scared and excited whilst I ran round the room a bit. There's an animal reaction to these things. The realisation we live on something much bigger than ourselves and of which we are a tiny part. Shakespeare knew all about it. About land, elements and story. (Although 'Blow winds and crack your cheeks' still makes me laugh in a wonderfully puerile way.) We sat

105

in animated chatter – as did the birds outside – for about an hour. All, indeed, did seem 'out of joint'.

I put the telly back on to its silly stand and pretty soon reports and exclamations came through of an earthquake hitting England measuring 5.2 on the Richter Scale. I felt a bit sad really. Something special happens and it's on the news within the hour. No mystery. No delight. No 'fair is foul', no wonder, no fear. No dance with the heavens. No elemental feeling. No affirmation. No story. Just another news story.

From where I live on the Welcombe Hills overlooking Stratford, I can see the spire of Holy Trinity Church, where Shakespeare is buried, and very often it is lit up, like an upturned ice-cream cone, to usher in the tourists. As my nerves settled after the shaking of the earth, and the last of the wine in my glass remained still, I turned the TV and its news stories off.

I looked out of my window at the shining spire in the wine-dark sky, and thought it must have been the Old Boy turning in his grave…

27 February 2008
(Afternoon)

TODAY, Wednesday 27th February, is our Birthday. We are two. And that is a big cause for celebration. WAHEY!!!!!! None of us have ever been in this situation before. We are in unchartered territory.

It seems it has passed in a flash, but so much has happened, so much to tell – and to feel, remember, rejoice – that it feels like a little lifetime. Indeed, talking of little lifetimes, Forbes brought in his beautiful ten month-old daughter this morning and she wasn't even a twinkle in her father's eye when we started this job. Some of us have lost parents, some of us have got married. Others have fallen in love. Others have fallen out of love. It's all here.

And we are STILL bloody rehearsing. Sigh. After two days off, following one of the hardest weeks in this whole two years, we are in understudy technical rehearsals for *Henry VI Part III*. Tonight we do *Richard II* for the first time in nearly a month. We do two shows tomorrow, then understudy techs for *Richard III* all day Friday; a performance of *Henry V* in the evening, then a nice little Trilogy Day on Saturday. And a wee Dickie Three on Sunday.

Nuts. Absolutely nuts. But, what a laugh! Time, as I've said before about this crazy job, is a relative concept. Two years. Blimey.

Talking of laughs, not content with putting in 12-hour days for the last month or whatever it is, we staged a special fund-raising Histories Cabaret on Sunday evening which went wonderfully. All the acts came from the Histories Family and were fantastic, and a big thank you to everyone who not only took part, but came and paid and helped raise so much money for Hannah's mother who has Multiple Sclerosis. We can now start work on lowering her kitchen so she can make a cup of tea in the morning and cook and wash up. It is fantastic news. And news to which I shed a tear when, next day, Hannah told her Mam how much we'd raised and heard the reaction. You all made a difference. Thank you.

Which is another cause for celebration today as well as our birthday! Again, we must all be looking forward and striving to be better and all the things that form part of our practice, and never rest on our laurels, but we can give ourselves a mighty pat on the back too.

Worth a couple or three in the Duck at least...

I T'S 4.45 pm on Friday 29 February 2008. Perhaps it's somehow appropriate that it takes this extra day of the year to achieve what's just happened. WE HAVE JUST FINISHED REHEARSING FOR THE LAST TIME.

It has been 2 years and 2 days. BLIMEY!!!!!!!!!!!!!!! From now on we will be performing and performing. Come London and the Roundhouse, yes we'll be doing techs and notes and the like, but we'll be fitting in understudy technicals alongside principal techs so it all goes like clockwork.

We finished just now the understudy tech rehearsal of *Richard III*, and there was a totally impromptu noise, which rumbled and grew rather like the earthquake that rattled us a couple of nights ago, emanating from somewhere deep within the heart of all us – cast and crew alike. It grew to a roar as we just shouted and bellowed a cry of victory, relief and exalted knackeredness. No one could quite believe it! I still can't now.

We have the small matter of performing *Henry V* this evening, so Julius now has to get his understudy head out of *Richard III* and become Bardolph. I have to stop slithering around as Catesby and become Pistol and Geoffrey has to step out of King Edward IV's ghostly shoes and become *Henry V* – a dynastic somersault if ever there was one. And then we have a Trilogy Day to do tomorrow! In at 9.15 for a half-hour-long fight call of all the *Henry VI* fights.

Silly. Very silly. But so, so gratifying. In the pub last night after *Henry IV Part II*, I met quite a few people who are seeing all eight shows this week. They are on

this extraordinary journey with us and it's such a joy to
feel as though we are all, actors and audiences alike,
on this big bus. This week is the first time in 400 years
that these eight History Plays of William Shakespeare
have been performed by one troupe of actors IN THEIR
ENTIRETY in succession. Performing them, I get the
real sense that it is not just another show. You can't
possibly just turn up and 'phone in' your performance.
The commitment from the audience (financially as
well as spiritually, I would imagine) matches our total
involvement over the last two years and it feels very,
very special.

And for us to be rehearsing at the same time as
all that is a bit nuts, but had to be done. And we've
finished. On a day that happens once every four years.

Huh, that's nothing – for The Histories, try once
every 400 years

WELL, we've just done EIGHT different shows   4 March 2008
in 5 days. (With two, day-long, understudy
technical rehearsals thrown in for good measure). What
an amazing journey it was.

Everyone had a story to tell. What happened when;
who dried; who corpsed; who could barely drag
themselves out of bed on Saturday morning to do three
shows (everybody); who could barely remember his
own name come the end of *Part III* that night; and again
the following morning when waking with a headache
sponsored by Flowers' Bitter and a mouthful of carpet
(me).

The reception we got on Saturday night after the
trilogy of the *Henry VIs* and again after *Richard III* on

Sunday was quite wonderful. Very memorable and emotional too. I have written before about how the show somehow comes with us into the pub. Well, on Saturday I'd say a good 95% of the people in the Duck had either sat through, crewed, or performed three plays that day and done 4 more in the few days before that. There was a palpable sense of joy and achievement and celebration. Just like a wedding party, in fact. We were definitely aggregating all over the place. Heady stuff. Well, that's what I felt on Sunday morning.

During *Richard III* on Sunday, people were coming offstage having done their last major bit with arms aloft in triumph and achievement – like marathon runners breaking the tape. But to be greeted with a standing ovation like the ones we received on Saturday and on Sunday is not everyday stuff and I will treasure them always.

When I was out of work as an actor, I used to play piano in bars, clubs and very, very posh hotels to pay the rent. I have spent hundreds, thousands, of hours playing away to people who are not listening. I once played 'Baa Baa Black Sheep' in every key, major and minor, for 45 minutes and nobody noticed. I even went through the whole of 'The Dark Side of the Moon' by Pink Floyd in a hotel lobby one evening just to see if anybody cared. (Although I loved it.)

I could've been Mozart sat there twiddling, and they would still have slouched there looking all fleshy, eating their scented peanuts and rattling their jewellery, and they may have heard it but not listened to it. I started thinking about that as 1000 people from all walks of life who had paid a lot of hard-earned money rose on Sunday to applaud us. And themselves. And the occasion. I thought about how much they HAD

listened. How much they had watched and thought and
followed us every step of the way.

A thousand people laughing when you say a
funny line is one of the truly great experiences.
What is getting a 'laugh'? I suppose it is the ultimate
feedback that you're doing OK and they're listening.
Corroboration? Collaboration? Truth? Recognition? But
the same thing can happen when you can hear a pin
drop in the audience. There you are on stage and the
audience are totally with you, eager, listening, aware.
It's very special. And is a testimony to that fantastic
space – The Courtyard – and not to me but to US. All
of US in that darkened room – the actors, the audience
and the crew. To the Plays. To the occasion; the project.
And that is the hair-raising, goose-pimply thing that
theatre can and should be.

Acting, art, is nothing if not communication. If it
doesn't do that, then it just becomes showing off. Or
background noise. I may well have given my best work
to a load of overpaid businessmen in bad suits in a
hotel in Piccadilly, maybe not. But I wasn't showing off.
And yet, I suspect I'm doing my best work in front of
1000 people every night and hopefully communicating
and not showing off. I am truly privileged. And that's
why there was a tear in my eye in the curtain calls on
Saturday and Sunday and why, through a glass lightly, I
went and got thoroughly slaughtered afterwards.

And my head still hurts. But in a good way.

A S Geoffrey Streatfeild (playing William Pole, Duke of Suffolk) restrains me towards the end of the Temple Garden scene in *Henry VI Part I* on Thursday night, Clive Wood as Richard Plantagenet says to me as Somerset, 'For your partaker, Pole, and you yourself/ I'll note you in my book of memory/ To scourge you for this apprehension/ Look to it well and say you are well warned.'

Now, whether it was just because we'd just had three days off (an unaccustomed and strange feeling – like bears waking too early from hibernation), or whether it was the prospect of doing three shows the next day and another three shows the day after that and finishing off with a quick *Henry V* on Sunday, I don't know, but my own 'book of memory' started going on the blink and instead of replying with: 'Ah, thou shalt find us ready for thee still…', I actually started saying Clive's final line – my understudy lines, lest ye not forget – before he did.

Odd.

Very alarming. I was there, I was in the scene, it was going well, I was in character and then suddenly out of nowhere I start saying my arch-enemy's lines.

As it was, my brain kicked in again and thought 'Heyup, something a tad wrong there'; my arse tightened a little; and I ended up just making a strange noise like someone with a bad cold and a dodgy stomach. Which, as readers will know, is neither uncommon or unusual in my world. Off I shot in my own lines – with a faintly quizzical look from Geoffrey who was clutching me by the shirt collar and was within earshot – and I was back on it.

Combine that with cutting the same Geoffrey off in the middle of his speech at the start of the scene, to which he responded with a hurt look and the fingering of his knife (which, incidentally, he has not let me forget for the last five shows), this mad 'eight different

shows in four days' business is all going rather well
for me.

It's certainly a great ride. We're performing, this
weekend, in the order in which Shakespeare wrote
them, so as I write, it's *Henry IV Part I* on Saturday
(our second Trilogy Day in a row), and it's my play
off. I can hear through the tinny Tannoy the shouts
and claps, laughs and thrills of Gadshill unfolding and
reverberating through the corridors backstage. Matt
Costain has just run past, panting and sweating, having
thrown himself off the lighting rig on a bungee rope.
The nutter.

Zoe the Stage Manager's voice echoes as she quietly
puts out calls for people to stand by for their entrances;
for stage staff to ready themselves for a cue; for Wigs to
standby with blood, Wardrobe to get ready for a quick
change. The hushed, ready, busy, breathless sound of a
theatre backstage.

So many people are working back here. All for one
end – to get the show(s) on. For the 35 actors that swan
about on the stage, there are 30 or 40 backstage staff
working very, very hard. At the end of each show there
is a huge press into action of all the technical staff in
order to set up for the next show.

All the lights are checked, the sound is levelled, the
ropes get checked for safety, the trapezes tested. The
props are changed, blood is set, wigs removed from
their boxes and combed, costumes wheeled in and
out, the props and socks and shirts of every actor set in
their place. They were here till 1am last night changing
around and were in again at 8 this morning to set up
for the three shows today. They are all as much a part of
this ensemble as any actor that struts and frets his hour
upon the stage. They are the best at what they do, and
they very, very rarely make a mistake. They're brilliant.

As actors, not only do we have to trust and rely on them – but we literally in some cases have to trust them with our lives. When you're fifty feet up clipped onto a ladder, covered in blood, sweating and confused about which way is up because you've been tumbling upside down, then the smiley face of Dave looming out the darkness (horrific vision in any other situation), ready with carabinas and safety, is a welcome sight. And I'm sure no one's ever said that about Dave before…

I think it shows how closely we all work together that some of the guys performed in the Cabaret we did a couple of weeks ago despite being as knackered as we were.

Geoffrey's just come offstage and sauntered past me wondering whether I might like to go on stage and cut a few of his lines again. But before I could reply, Zoe's put the call out to standby for the interval, so the backstage world will change for fifteen minutes. I'm off, I say. Have a good second half. See you for *Part II*. Already, stage crew dressed in black are rushing past, ready to sweep the stage or set a prop.

This is my world and I love it. I can hear the seashell sound of the audience, clapping.

18 March 2008

GLORIOUSLY, we finished. And what a way to leave Stratford, The Courtyard, our friends and our houses and cottages and rivers and fields and birthplaces and building sites. We did what's been billed as 'The Glorious Moment'. We did it. And so did the audience. *Richard II* through to *Richard III* in four days with two trilogy days back to back. Hardcore.

It is almost impossible to pick out individual moments – it all seems like a bit of a blur. But for us, there were one or two glorious moments within the whole 'Glorious Moment' as it were. Moments when the heart skipped a beat and the world went into slow motion. The most apparent one, as people who were there will testify, was the moment in *Henry VI Part III* in Act 2 – the 'Parley' between the two opposing sides before the crucial Battle of Towton – when we ground to a rather rude halt and stood there in a sort of Mexican stand-off for 10 seconds or so, eyes darting about like Sergio Leone on acid. Eventually, Miles came to the rescue by coining a rough approximation of the lines and off we shot again, all of us slightly greyer of hair and browner of trouser. I'm sure everyone had their own mini-crises at some stage, but we all had a ball.

Every time I perform these shows I feel a pride, and get a feeling that something special is going on. Again, something remarkable happened over the last few days: our relationship with the audience. As actors, our brief is ostensibly to do the 'same' thing to a 'different' audience every night. This time we were doing a 'different' thing to the 'same' audience. And it proved wonderfully symbiotic.

Talking to people afterwards a common theme was that all had felt part of the company. Part of the show. We, as performers, felt this and responded accordingly. As a consequence, there was understanding. All the nuances, maturity, feeling, and sheer hard work we have put into these shows were all apparent. It is a great feeling, to share it.

What's more, we've been engaged on this project for two years and a lot of the audience have shared that journey in their own way with us. Which is ALL about what Michael is trying to achieve as Artistic

Director of this place. Acting, theatre, performance is not exclusive. It is inclusive. So the standing ovation which we got on Sunday evening (which I will always remember and even now, two days on, gives me goose bumps just thinking about) was not just the audience clapping us and saying well done; it felt like a genuine celebration of the whole building. Of us all. Not a patting on the back of each other mutual smugness, but a real arms-aloft joy. As the lights came up after the final blackout, we, the actors, just stood there on stage and were all taken aback by the reception. The noise, it was unbelievable. We just stood there some more. Eventually, we started to bow.

Theatre comes and goes as quickly as you can tell it. It exists in a moment. But, in a way, this has existed for two years. The Courtyard, that sweet blessed hull and hulk of a rusty shed, was built to express an idea and for these shows to live and breathe it. Also, as actors we are used to things being ephemeral. Our lives and our work. We are very good at getting to know people very quickly – you have to – because you are working, trusting, sharing with them the moment you meet. The flip-side is that we are used to saying goodbye very quickly – it doesn't make it any easier, but we are used to it. Gypsies. Travellers. But this is different.

We, as a company, took a lot longer than usual to get to know each other collectively because we knew we had the time. Consequently, our friendships and love for each other now go deeper and have firmer foundations. The same can be said of our relationship with The Courtyard, not just the theatre itself, but the people who work in it every day – the Front of House staff, the Green Room staff, the cleaners, technicians, the Box Office, the Café and Bar. It is a real wrench.

And the weird thing was that as we were performing these plays last weekend all the company were packing at the same time and so were the shows. As people went home at night, so they were packing their bags and emptying their fridges ready for the off. As each prop or piece of set was used for the last time, so they were packed away into the growing mountain of boxes in the massive back dock behind the stage. It sure socks it home to you that what you're doing is a point in time. I love and loathe it all at once.

But so much has happened. So much to tell. So much to remember. It's the reason why I started writing. To record. To make it less of a fleeting moment in time. Impossible, of course. You have to let go. That is why, as I bowed on Sunday night, and beamed a smile of pure pleasure, so I could feel my tears fall to the floor. But we had all shared a moment.

And it was glorious.

SPRING 2008
LONDON

THIS is the largest build for a show the RSC has ever undertaken. Teams of workers have been pouring like ants over the Roundhouse, day and night, to build an approximation of The Courtyard in 10 days: and we've still managed to find a place for the table tennis table. Result!

As Bartlett and Wood (a solid, often inspired, seasoned partnership) took on Streatfeild and Asbury (fiery, mercurial at times, and in my case frequently missing the target), in a hotly contested game of doubles, with Tom Piper the designer, refereeing, so the Roundhouse tech crew looked on dumbfound. Who are these guys? What the...? It made me smile.

The simple fact is that we are The Histories and we are here. And when I say The Histories, I mean the whole thing. All the crew, wardrobe, wigs, the lighting lads, the automation, set, ropes, ladders, bungees, slings and arrows; and the cauldron that is the auditorium. It's fantastic. The sails at the top, put there for the acoustics, put me in mind of the gladiatorial circuses in Rome.

The sheer logistical exercise of it is mind-boggling. They have done amazing feats in getting this thing in so quick. Two months ago we were given a tour of the auditorium that was being built in an industrial unit in Stratford. 23 articulated lorries took it all down here to London. And then they had to build it. It really is extraordinary. Peter Bailey, the project manager who made all this happen, is a magician.

And I love backstage. Or rather, behind the curtain. We are all lined up in booths of two all along the semicircle behind the back of the set which fits into the circular wall of the Roundhouse. There is literally a curtain between us and the audience. So that means that all the farts, wheezes, coughs and expectorations that make up the usual soundscape of a male dressing

room have to be tempered somewhat. It's actually quite
exciting. It's a lovely atmosphere – you get the feeling
that something special is going on. Like playing hide
and seek when you were a child. There is something
breathless to keeping quiet.

And the shows are really beginning to fit in here. As
I write, we are about to do a dress of *Henry IV Part
II*. *Richard II* went really well. I had to go and do the
mobile phone announcement thingy that we do these
days. So I guess I was the first person to speak on this
stage. I'm weirdly quite proud of that for some reason.
But it was quite interesting to see the rather blank looks
that I was greeted with. They are just not used to having
that sort of thing here in London. Still, we'll train them.
When you compare it to the feeling we shared with the
last audience two weeks ago in the Glorious Moment –
it certainly feels more distant. But that's only to be
expected. We will have our time here too.

As we will with the table tennis now that we've
found a little space for it. After two weeks off (although
a week of gastric flu didn't help) I'm well up for it. And
for putting on 8 shows.

I T'S Tuesday morning, we're about to do a Dress of
Henry V and then our first performance of it this
evening, and I can barely speak.

I came on as Pistol in *Henry IV Part II* on Saturday
night, towards the end of the play when Pistol breaks
the news to Falstaff and friends that the old King is
dead. I flew the through the balcony doors, looked at
David as Falstaff and hollered, 'Save you, Sir John!', and

0 April 2008

promptly felt as if someone with badly cut fingernails had scraped them down the inside of my throat. Just like that.

I got through to the end of the play. Sunday was spent filming, in a luckily silent role I might add, for a mate of mine's film in a freezing shed in Chiswick and then Monday we started teching for *Henry V*. I tried my best but after twelve hours of that the only noise I could make sounded like an old dog trying to bark. Or a badger attacking a bike.

It's because you can't do any impromptu warmup here. In *Henry IV Part II*, I come on all guns blazing as Pistol in the first half, and it's about an hour and a half later that I come back on at full tilt again. In that time the voice has warmed down and there's nowhere here to give it a quick limber up before you go on. In Stratford it's something I didn't even think about. You just do it – we're only talking twenty seconds of making silly noises and sounding like Eccles – but here unless you want seriously to put off the audience and, indeed, your fellow actors, you keep mumm. So it's a 'steamer' for me – that weird device that looks like some medieval torture: basically attaching your mouth to a boiling kettle as far I can see. Lots of gentle warming up all day, and a wing and a prayer.

But I do love it here. Our dressing room 'booths' become more hilarious every day. They stretch right around the semicircle backstage with the wardrobe department in the middle. There are two to a booth, and there is a real sense of community. It's like being in a caravan park on a summer's evening. You go past and each booth is identical but has its own identity and life within it. Because of the enforced silence, each has a certain sense of peace and quietness as if, like those achingly English campsites, no one wants to disturb anybody else.

Or again, because each booth is draped with two red curtains that meet in the middle to give some privacy if you want it, it somehow looks like a Moroccan street bazaar, with all the traders selling their wares – although, as Forbes pointed out, it looks more like the red light district in Amsterdam than anything else.

There have been a few teething problems, but the technical crew have done wonders. These guys have been putting in ridiculously long hours for weeks now and, because of their hard work, it seems to be going down a storm. I think. They seemed to clap at the end. Which is always a bonus. It's a bit unnerving sometimes when you're in full flow – as I was on Saturday night in *Part II* – and I looked into the audience and there was one lad looking more bored than I ever was in a Maths lesson and what I presume was his dad next to him, staring open-mouthed into the lighting grid. Kind of gees you up. I had to turn round and look at the other side of the audience just to see if anyone was interested. It goes with the territory of no fourth wall. You're in there with them and no matter how much they're enjoying it, there's always going to be someone shuffling in their seat and looking like a hostage. Still, there's always a few bangs and crashes to wake them up in these shows.

Given the state of my voice they'll soon perk up, wondering why an actor sounds like a badger, although I have a sneaking suspicion that it'll be fine – after all, there is always the lighting grid to look at.

THE flat I'm renting whilst in London overlooks The Roundhouse. Which is nice for the commute, but not so nice on Sunday when the first thing you see on your day off is your place of work. But, believe you me, I'm not complaining.

To live so close when you have a Trilogy Day the next day after having performed in the evening is a godsend. Some are having to get on the tube and train and bus to get home by midnight, then get up at sparrow's fart to be in again for a fight call at 9.15. That doesn't happen in Stratford.

Still, this morning I opened the curtains and saw a BBC transmission van outside the theatre, clicked on the telly and there was the set, my colleagues and friends in all their glory on BBC News 24. Another day, another story, another opening, another show. It's always weird when that happens. (Throwing open the curtains reminds me of a time about 7 years ago when I was doing *The Seagull* at Stratford and was staying in the legendary Room No 6 in The Ferryhouse – a room on the top floor of the RSC accommodation house right by the Stratford ferry, overlooking the road and the river. I got up, stark naked, and went to the window, pulling back the curtains with gusto to reveal not only a glorious day but one of those open-top tourist buses, stopped in traffic, crammed full of Japanese with their many cameras, looking straight at me at eye level. Well, not quite eye level, but you get what I mean. I stood there, *Life of Brian*-like for a stunned few seconds whilst they let out a series of exclamations and gasps. One reached for their camera. I took this as a cue to leave, and mustering all the dignity I could, flashed a smile, threw a devilish wave and hit the floor. I like to think they still talk of me from time to time. God knows what's in their photo collection.)

But seeing my working life on the telly gave
me a little frisson to start the day, which has only
continued -- through a friend ringing me up out of the
blue whom I showed around the theatre -- with the
palpable air of excitement, as there are cameras on set
and there is 'live' transmission. Which of course means
it's Press Night tonight. And tomorrow. But then that's
par for the course for this crazy project. The fact that
we do another Press Night/Day thingy in two weeks'
time with the Henry VIs and Richard III only adds to the
strangeness and wonder of it all.

I've written before about Press/Opening Night and the
slight heightening of senses. It seems quite strange now,
after two years and 2 months to be 'opening' a show –
ridiculous – but that's where we're at. Even so, there's
still the familiar tingle and the faint whiff of glamour as
cards, flowers and presents start arriving.

But it does also seem very silly now. And it's great.
We've been together so long and been through so much,
that to worry about press reviews and all the like is just
stupid. We have total faith in ourselves and each other
to be able to do the best we possibly can. Not cockiness
or arrogance. Just belief. And that's not just tonight but
every performance we do. This project has abnegated
the need for press approbation. We just get on with it
and it's very refreshing.

So whilst tonight and tomorrow will be special,
so it will be every night. As, in fact, every night has
been over the last two years of performing. The BBC
and their cameras will leave and we can get on with
lighting the imagination for that one moment in time
that theatre can do. (Or opening the curtains on a
second floor window in Stratford – which didn't leave
anything to the imagination, but was a moment in time,
I suppose.) And as we draw towards the end of May and

the end of our contract, so each night; each show; each meeting in the bar afterwards, will be not just special, but unforgettable.

WE had a day off after Press Day. Necessary, not least because I couldn't feel my face due to the ill-advised attempt to slake my thirst, after four shows in 24 hours, with free white wine at the Press Night Party. That, alongside a minor tête-à-tête with a Glaswegian in the bar over the road after the party, meant the shadow of my hangover had destroyed the shadow of my face that day.

And then, Friday, we were back into technicals for *Henry VI Part I*. It's hanging off a ladder twenty feet up covered in blood time again! It took us from 10 in the morning till 10 at night to get that show into here; then we had a Dress Rehearsal on Saturday, and did the show that night. If you include 2000/1 when we first staged the *Henry VI*s, these are the seventh techs I've done for these shows – if you include all the understudy techs then it's twelve. Another fact I'm weirdly proud of.

In the Dress Rehearsal, in the scene where Henry is crowned in Paris, and York challenges Somerset to a fight, we had an almost cast-wide corpse. Everyone present on stage just started giggling. It had started when Cordery mistimed picking up the gauntlet thrown down by York and ended bobbing up and down like a yo-yo trying to pick it up. A silly, small thing, but that is the manner of corpsing – it's the tiny out of the ordinary things that set you off. This time, Clive Wood, who's particularly good at not corpsing, just lost it. There were tears streaming down his face with suppressed laughter. Chuk, after emitting strange sounds, simply turned upstage and doubled over. Streatfeild used the letter from the Duke of Burgundy to cover his face.

I was making noises again. I couldn't see because of the tears and what made it worse was that Cordery's voice had risen an octave as he fought back the gagging. It was as if all the effort and pent-up emotions of putting all the first four plays on over the last few weeks were pouring out of us. It WAS a dress, so it wasn't too bad to do it and we, as a company, just laughed and laughed in the place which is most dear to us – on that stage. Lovely.

As have been the reviews, apparently. As I said about Press Night last week, it all seems rather strange to be 'opening' a show two years in. It shows what an ensemble can do, I suppose.

But, in truth, I'm much more interested in what a Casting Director or Director thinks of the shows. They're the ones who are going to give me a job. And it is to those people we are looking now. That icy hand of unemployment is not just fingering our collar, but grabbing it and pushing us towards the door like the bouncer did to me in the bar over the road on Press Night. The rollercoaster is back. It's been at its very zenith for the past nearly three years and I'm fearful there's another dip around the corner.

Although I'm sure it'll never be as bad as it was at its lowest point. I remember doing DRACULA, or How's Your Blood, Count? on tour in 1996. I was Acting ASM (Assistant Stage Manager who does a spot of acting – I'm not sure you even get those anymore), and by the end of the show I was playing a transvestite vampire, wearing a PVC Basque, fishnet stockings and boots. As you can imagine, a show like that was immensely popular and they had sold, oooh, about seventeen tickets in a thousand-seat theatre in Southend. So, joy of joys, they threw open the theatre to all the local schools.

You can imagine I was overjoyed, knowing what costume I was wearing. There I was standing in all that garb, growling or whatever idiotic thing I was supposed to be doing, hearing the whoops and hollers of about 500 crazed and nonplussed Southend schoolkids ringing about the theatre, when I was hit in the eye by a Chewit. Some little tyke had got me. I stood there, bolt upright, hand clasped to my left eye, while the other swivelled frantically, trying to find the culprit in the darkness of the audience. '**** this,' I said and walked off stage rather stiffly.

That, dear readers, was a low, low point. Although, of course, not even that compares to the long days of unemployment watching *Neighbours* (twice, when you could), and you have to count up your coppers just to pop to the corner shop.

Which is why I will always laugh when I'm onstage and working. Why this has been such a special project for me, and for us all, is that we have achieved that nirvana state of security, and thus have been able to blossom. Long may it last into our new work and lives after this job. I know that, without arrogance or cockiness, I can walk into any audition or job with my head held high and a belief in myself. The gossamer thread which keeps us from the dark days has got stronger with this job, and we'll be better in the big bad acting world outside because of it.

But, Casting Directors, please note, I'm never wearing fishnets again.

T HREE and a half weeks to go till the lights go out
and the next day someone comes in with a huge
angle grinder and cuts this set to pieces and sells it on
for scrap metal. Which breaks my heart, quite frankly.

30 April 2008

And might be quite a good analogy for my career,
who knows? Sigh. Still, my brother is a blacksmith,
and lives in a tiny little village in Herefordshire where
I grew up, and is quite good at welding things back
together again. A few of us were thinking he might
be able to get the metal sheets which cover the stage
and, along with cutting up a few ladders, could cobble
together some coffee tables or something out them. You
never know.

But the main talk all around the cast is of Casting
Directors, Agents, auditions and scripts. Who's in the
audience, who's not, whose mare's dead. It's a shame,
but inevitable. We face the future standing on brittle
metal. There's always someone ready with an angle
grinder. You may well say, and you would be right,
that we have reached the RSC, one of the pinnacles of
our profession; been involved with one of the greatest
projects it has ever staged; lived, laughed and loved
under the most secure roof any actor could wish for;
become better as an actor, as a person; strived to be
better. All of which is truer than I could possibly relate,
but that makes the fear of leaving and of what will
happen next, on occasion, somehow more extreme.
Other times, it seems absolutely fine. As I have said,
we can walk from here with our heads held high. But
inevitably, given our chosen profession, the vagaries of
employment are an important topic of conversation.
Only two of us have a job come the end of May – and
one of those is a day's filming on *Little Dorrit*...

But, onwards and upwards. In the bar after the
show every night there are usually one or two agents

hovering about with one of their clients having been in the show, accompanied by Casting Directors and the like. I never know who they are, or indeed what to say ('Er… Give us a job?') but it's all a good sign. Last night, as well as a girl who broke my heart years ago, the place was teeming with them. It's always the mark of a successful 'London' show: people you haven't seen for ages suddenly start appearing.

Business-wise, it's a sign that these shows are a great calling card. I'm inordinately proud of them and everybody in it: I will be very proud when they get jobs and I go see them in things. For the main thing is that, even though in three weeks' time we shall be splitting up, we will always be a group. They can break my heart by cutting up the set. Girlfriends can too. But we can always say, 'We did this.' And wherever go, whatever we do, we will always be part of something, not parted. A band of brothers and sisters. With metal coffee tables. Made by my other brother.

Tough on the heart this business.

1 May 2008

NO matter how down you can get, you can always rely on old Dr Theatre to cheer you up. Now, I'm aware that I sound like an old ham here, but last night's performance of *Henry VI Part I* was just one of those shows.

I love performing it, anyway, but a few things happened that made me smile. Firstly, I got blown off the ladder as Salisbury and am busy dying, all covered in blood, and hanging 20 feet off the ground, when I remember a note that Michael gave me when he told me to stop 'dying' so much. Let the image do the work.

He was right, but I always love that bit because it takes me back to being an eight year old and practising being shot whilst standing on my bed. Man, I was better than James Bond back then. Anyway, it flits through my mind as I'm hamming it up for England, and I stop shivering, shaking, fitting, gargling and my mind goes into a little blank and I just let out a strange noise like Frankie Howerd on a bad day.

'Ooooooheeeehooohmmmmmnngghoo...', I go. And at once Chris McGill, who is on the same ladder as me and supposed to be consoling my imminent death, lets out an audible yelp, grabs my head and clasps it to him as he bursts into suppressed laughter. I'm so surprised myself that I start giggling too, and pretty soon the whole ladder's shaking for all the wrong reasons, and Keith Bartlett as Talbot is busy banging on about my one eye shining at the sun or whatever he says, and looking like Mad Eye Moody at us. I get dragged out into the flies and eventually put out of my misery by the two Daves up in the gods, to whom I trust my life on a nightly basis, giving me questioning looks.

I then have to do a mad dash down the flights of crazily thin stairs erected just behind the set – which, when you've got one eye and half your face covered in blood and a back scabbard on, is no mean feat a) to survive, and b) to survive quietly – and rush to the quick change area. Wipe off said blood, take off the Salisbury costume, put on an English Soldier costume, run round just in time to carry on a ladder from downstage left with Kieran, pull him up to the ladder, chant a bit, pull down a blue silk, run off (last night avoiding Clive as he came a cropper on someone's silk and landed square on his hip and elbow with a loud expletive right in front of the only school kids in the audience), and then rush upstairs to change into the Duke of Somerset's cossie whilst sweating like George

Bush playing Scrabble. Then it's rush downstairs,
a second or two to get myself together, shout a bit
when all Talbot's soldiers swing across to ambush the
Countess d'Auvergne, and then, whoosh, we're on into
the Temple Garden scene.

This is the scene where all the protagonists pick
white or red roses thereby setting in action all the
events leading to the so-called Wars of the Roses.
I storm on, all annoyed with Clive as Richard
Plantagenet, being restrained by Geoffrey as Suffolk,
when I notice that Geoffrey's wearing a metal red rose,
left on his costume from the last time we did the show.
Obviously this kind of pre-empts the scene. So I mutter
out of the side of my mouth 'You've got a bloody rose
on,' at which, cool as a cucumber, Geoffrey lets me go;
storms upstage towards Clive and, a brief but miniscule
swipe at his own chest later, turns round to me to say
his line and the offending article is gone. God knows
where he put it. We exchange a bit of eyebrow-raising
and I hold down a brief snigger and we're off. Ah,
Doctor Stage.

Then later in the second half over the dead, prostrate
bodies of Talbot and his son young John, Katy, instead
of saying 'I think this upstart is Old Talbot's ghost', says,
'I think this upstart is Old Galbot's toast'. This not only
reduced the listening French Army to tears, but left
Keith and Lex – Talbot and son respectively – in the
unenviable position of corpsing whilst being a corpse.
They just could not move whilst inside both of them
were screaming. I saw them when they came offstage
and Keith's head had nearly exploded. He was purple.
Lex was doubled over in pain. Such little things are the
stuff of nightmares and dreams.

Then Tom has a mental blip and seriously has to
ask Geoffrey what came first, the burning of Joan or
the wooing of Margaret? Which if anybody knows

these shows, is a bit of a major slip up. He was gently reminded that the actress playing Margaret plays Joan as well, who has to die before Margaret appears, and told to go sit down and have long hard think about things.

Poor chap, it could've been any one of us, such is the schedule we've been working to in the last month. And, however up and down the rollercoaster goes, it's evenings like last night that will always keep me going and keep me on a level. Means I can enjoy the rush as my stomach churns with the loop-the-loop.

■

TOWARDS the end of *Henry VI Part II* last night, as the Duke of Somerset, I try and arrest Clive as the Duke of York for treason. 2 May 2008

His sons come on, all swords and ambush, and I'm left there standing helpless as Clive picks out my dagger and slowly puts it up my nose and then slits my nostril. I get to think I'm Jack Nicholson in *Chinatown* and, if we do it right, the audience get to wince a bit. Over the last few weeks I've never got the blood quite right. I have a little blood bag in my left hand and when Clive pulls back the knife I give it a squeeze and hey presto there's blood all over my nose and the left side of my face. More often than not though, I give the blood bag a squeeze and the damn stuff shoots off at right angles and, on a couple of occasions, has artfully decorated the dresses of some of the audience in the front row. Last night, however, I'd worked out a little routine where I was sure it wasn't going to go wrong. I followed it to the letter. It went well. Too well. As I squeezed, the lot went straight up my nose. At the same time, I was busy acting away and snorted in rather than out.

I hit the deck as I usually do, this time snorting outwards like a flu victim. I could feel it all travelling about my head, tingling and burbling. I got up gingerly and luckily didn't have to say anything else in the rest of the scene apart from stand there all moodily – except this time I was standing there with tears streaming down my face looking like a bulldog sucking a wasp.

Then, joy of joys, it empties from my sinuses and starts descending to the back of my throat – whereupon I start gagging and retching involuntarily. I just about make it to the end of the scene. I run off and at the back of the audience downstage right, grab a basketful of wet towels, throw them out, and start vomiting and heaving up fake blood. I tried to time it with the drums on stage, but it must have been faintly disturbing to hear from the other side of the wooden panel when you're trying to watch a show.

Katy, who started basic training as a paramedic once, nearly went into an emergency drill as she came off stage and saw me hard it, doubled over emitting blood. Then I had to run round to stage left, and put on my leather breastplate. Fran, one of our genius Stage Management, who by this time had been alerted by Jenny from Wigs (who was warily eyeing the towel tray I'd just hoicked into), brought me a glass of water, God bless her, and then I had to put another huge blood bag in my mouth and go and fight with Slinger as the young Richard, where I get killed and spit blood all over his face. I was in quite a rush to get off at the end of the fight, so apparently he lifted my right leg and I lifted my left leg for him to drag me off, which is always nice of a dead body, I feel.

I was coughing up blood all last night every now and then, and it must've dribbled out of my nose during the night, because my pillow looked like a pizza when I woke up. And my landlady was looking askance at me later on. Such are the joys of The Histories.

There's always a price to pay for thinking you're Jack Nicholson, if only for a second.

I DIDN'T write at all last week, firstly because it was Press Day and Night for the *Henry VIs* and *Richard III*, and secondly because I caught one in Barnet.

15 May 2008

No, this is not the story of a dodgy encounter at the end of the Northern Line. I got smacked over the bridge of my right hand in the Battle of Barnet. This, let me remind you, is the fight towards the end of *Henry VI Part III* when Warwick is killed and fifteen guys with broadswords fight on the stage at the same time. It's bloody dangerous at the best of times.

Each move of the sword and body is carefully choreographed by the master, Terry King, so that it is safe, but mishaps can happen. I got a sword round the shoulder about two years ago doing the same fight and others have had little nicks and near misses (which could be the title of my autobiography). It almost invariably comes at the end of a very long day of performance, so minds and bodies are tired. Suffice to say I got a sword right across my hand at full wallop.

I shot off stage in some distress. I thought it was broken to be honest – God, it hurt. I took my glove off and there was a small, very deep hole in my hand, but I could feel it wasn't broken. Then I found myself in the odd position of having to put fake blood and mud on my face whilst real blood was streaming from my hand. Odd, I thought. Then I had to put my glove back on –

no mean feat as my hand had already swelled up, rush back onstage and shout 'Ah, Warwick, Warwick…!' and look all concerned and pained about poor old Patrice, playing the Earl of Warwick, all a-dying and making strange high-pitched noises.

The pained I could do, concerned frankly less so. Finally, he died, which meant I was able to pelt off stage and let out a silent scream. Then it was on to support Katy as Margaret in her speech, then warble on about 'owls by day' or something, then rush off and get really bloodied up with a bag over my head ready to get told I'm to lose said head by Forbes as Edward IV. Phew.

One of my most treasured moments in this project is standing in the 'Hell Mouth' (the mirrored area behind the big double doors upstage centre) before that last entrance in *Part III*. It is pitch black back there, and the boys are going mental on the drums up above us while Chuk, as Henry VI, wanders about in falling feathers on stage. The noise, it's incredible. It seems to be amplified by the tunnel that we're all crammed together in, and it never fails to stir the soul. I love it.

This time however I was concentrating on getting a piece of rope over my throbbing hand. Suddenly we burst out of the doors like water from a sewer and I spit at Forbes (which came out as a dry sort of sphutt because I'd lost all saliva), say a few choice words, then I'm off – thank God.

It's my last exit of the day and as I hear the awful, fearful sounds of Katy in full cry at the death of her son, I'm finally able to take off my glove and inspect the damage. I'll live – but I couldn't write for three days. And the worst thing was, because it was Press Day, at the party afterwards everyone kept shaking my hand and I'd start bowing, my knees buckling, and I'd be making a noise like Fu Manchu. Man, the weird stares I got. I was introduced to some posh Casting Director

and I'm sure I'll get an audition for the next martial arts
epic...

But, in truth, we're beginning to hurt ourselves rather a
lot. It's because we're tired and we're pushing ourselves,
and maybe, just maybe, it's because we know it's all
coming to an end soon. Katy fell off the stage during the
Death of York scene in *Part III*. She popped back up and
in Clive's words looked like a meerkat as she remained
where she was in the audience and carried it off with
aplomb. He was kneeling there trying to do his death
speech and that was all he could think of. But she really
hurt herself. The bruise on her hip looks like Jupiter
and the scrape up her entire arm's length is not funny.

Both Richard Cordery and David Warner walked
slap bang into the metal posts backstage and came away
with Tom & Jerry-like bumps. We had another Trilogy
Day on Saturday, and I ended up falling into the trap as
Pistol during the fight with Falstaff – doing my knee in
at the same time.

I'm aware that I'm sounding like the biggest
hypochondriac in the world here, but it's bizarre.
Then again, everything is bizarre in this job. We've
just done a Press Night and we end in two weeks. We
have two octologies in a row. That in itself is a serious
undertaking.

But then we stop.

We've just had three days off, which is lovely,
although rather stupidly I played my first game of
cricket of the season on Sunday and consequently
couldn't move for two days. We have spent two and a
half years jumping and running through a series of ever
bigger hoops. Just two more to go. And we'll try not to
hurt ourselves.

I think it's the getting through the last hoop that will hurt the more.

■

IN Towton – the Battle in *Henry VI Part III* staged using all the ropes – I get to climb the upstage right ladder, flail around a bit all angsty and injured, then fall back to earth fetching up with my leg hung artfully over the bottom rung of the ladder and fall asleep for twenty minutes.

It's a spectacular death, which in truth I defy anyone to have ever seen, as there's lots more interesting things going on elsewhere – namely various suicidal actors throwing themselves about on ropes and falling from the gods or whatever. I'm doing what I'm doing merely just to get on and be a dead body for a long, long time. The Molehill speech of *Henry VI*; the father who killed his son and the son who killed his father; the dying speech of Clifford; the dismembering of Clifford by the York brothers – all take place whilst Hannah, Alexia, Geoffrey Streatfeild, John Mackay and myself lie there trying not to move. Geoffrey even gets sat upon. Oh, the indignity. Now that's ensemble.

I'm telling you it's not easy. The feet start to cramp and if you even get one limb slightly out of place at the start, you're going to be regretting it in two minutes, let alone twenty. Pins and needles set in. Your face starts to feel like blancmange. And to cap it all, some other bloody actor might come along and tread on your fingers – which happened about two years ago. I had my eyes closed at the time so I still don't know who it was, but I have my suspicions. And palpably I haven't forgotten. Those fingers make me good money when I'm not busy lying around a stage...

But, after two years, we're getting pretty good at it. Indeed, so good am I that I'm fast asleep by the end of the Molehill speech. And certainly when we're doing this crazy octology I found, to my shame, that I was rather looking forward to it. It's the only time I get a bit of horizontal time in the whole thing.

As I write, it's Sunday and we are about to do *Richard III* for the penultimate time. We have just done seven different shows in three days. Yesterday was so exhilarating and knackering. I don't know about anybody else but I found it very hard. But, like everything I suppose, the more we pushed ourselves the more we got out of it. However, by the time Towton came along on *Part III*, I was ready for a kip.

In days gone by I would always love to keep half an eye open and watch the audience as I lay there. Or listen to the sounds. Just listening to theatre can be very exalting sometimes. But I'd love seeing the grimaces on the audience's faces when Clifford gets cut up. Seeing the tears appear in their eyes when Chuk does his speech, or Keith and Lex realise they've killed one another. But in the height of an octology, you grab rest wherever you can get it.

The trick, of course, is to fall asleep not only in the right position to be comfortable, but also to shield any involuntary movements you might make whilst asleep. It's like falling asleep whilst watching a show: you have to make sure your head lolls forward, because if it tips back, not only are you advertising to the world your disinterested state, but as the head goes so your mouth drifts downwards and you let out a rasping back of the throat snore which could break windows at forty paces. Or is that just me?

Needless to say, I always wake up on cue. Honest. The trick there, obviously, is not to wake up with a start. It wouldn't do suddenly to jolt upright with a short exclamation and a percussive fart. Not when you're dead. You've got to glide in and out of consciousness like you're on a train looking out of the window. It's an art.

Of course, it takes practice to make perfect. Perhaps it's because I'm a musician, but I've always maintained that acting, like any other art form, is a craft. It takes constant practice, which needs to be maintained, honed and perfected. And you can't do that sitting at home on the sofa, waiting for the phone to ring. It's why people who start getting work early in their career very often keep on working, as they get the chance constantly to be doing it and get better. You could have someone with exactly the same talent, if not more, but with a different face who doesn't quite get a lot of jobs early on and then falls into that cycle of not doing it enough, losing confidence and being left behind.

It's tough. Which is exactly what Michael is trying to avoid with this notion of ensemble and bigger contracts. The idea that actors perform better with the threat of penury hanging over them needs to be challenged. Within this job we have grown, all of us. Become better actors. And it feels great. To know that we're getting somewhere.

But in a week's time we will all be splitting up and drifting off into the ocean. I was talking to a member of the audience last night and they just could not believe that. They somehow thought that all this energy – all this talent – should somehow be harnessed into something more.

And it does feel weird. But what I hope is that we as individuals – we'll always be together in spirit – will harness all of that energy and take it into our next jobs, our ensuing lives. Even if it's just knowing how to sleep without moving. I'm working on the snoring. Practice makes perfect.

Talking of that, I can hear Jon Slinger beginning to warm up for the show which starts in two hours' time. I can feel the theatre beginning to wake from its own slumber this afternoon.

And suddenly, I don't want it to stop.

THERE'S a point that musicians get to when, after many years of practice – in my case, hours and hours of sitting twiddling away at the piano as a teenager – they say that the instrument begins to 'play itself'.

24 May 2008

As a jazz musician, it's certainly the case. You don't think of what you're going to play next, how the expression of a bar or phrase will go, how it will sound. You just play. And the piano 'plays itself' because the brain doesn't get in the way. The filter that judges things as a performer starts to switch off and you become very present. It's why at rock and jazz gigs that 'presence' is communicated to the audience and they feel able to (and should) whoop out and holler and scream when said rock god is up and strutting his stuff i.e. playing – up on stage.

Why be an actor, then? One of the very many great things about doing an Octology is that performers and audiences alike, either through tiredness and concentration, or a combination of both, become over the course of eight plays locked into each other in the very present. The plays start 'playing themselves'. Only what is happening on stage and what the character (and therefore the audience) is feeling matters at that point.

That is true play. The ability to lose oneself in a world full of imagination and without a care for anything else apart from what happens in that moment.

The plays and the performers have to be good, of course. Imagine sitting through some turkey of a show for four days. Well, the answer is, you wouldn't, and it wouldn't last very long. But maybe because we've been together for so long and worked so hard to be better, hopefully we're doing OK and we start having that relationship with the audience. This, surely, is best practice.

And it's not just restricted to a publicly funded theatre company. There are ensembles all over the country doing great work from Dundee Rep to Colchester with many others in between. (I'd love to experiment somehow doing the same ensemble idea with film. The only example I can think of that has a similar ensemble feel, where actors continuously appeared in differing roles in a succession of films, are the *Carry On* films. Maybe it's time to try.)

But if there is one abiding memory I will take from the Octology we did last week, it is the woman in the second row, stage left, who at the Curtain Call for *Richard III* was standing, tears streaming from her face, smiling, clapping and cheering, covered from her right shoulder to her left hip in a furious line of blood, spurted from Richard III (Jon) as he was killed by the Earl of Richmond (Lex). I love that. It's from little moments like this that convince me in my fonder moments that we're about to enter a Golden Age of Theatre over the next forty or so years. As the world becomes ever more virtual and the computer and television break into every thread of our lives, so the thrill of someBODY actually standing there in front of you, sweating, muddied and bloodied, crying over the death of his son, can become even more of an event

than it already is. The thrill of the ritual, the story. The
threshold point. The excitement of community. Things
happen to you in a theatre – from getting covered
in a Zorro-like trail of blood to seeing people fling
themselves at each other on ropes; to people actually
speaking AT you.

It is so wondrous to see the faces of people during
the shows – and especially at the curtain call after eight
shows – lit with delight, wonder and joy. Clapping.
Cheering. God knows what our faces must look like.
Similar, I think. We've all of us in that room been on
a journey and we've played. It is humbling, joyous
and emotional – the release of so much love and
appreciation.

And, for a second, only for a silly second, I start
feeling like a rock god… Only joking, actually I feel
the proudest actor alive. And with only one more set of
eight to go, that decision I made when I was sixteen to
be an actor, not a musician, has borne more fruit than I
could possibly imagine.

I'm very, very lucky.

IT'S half past eleven on Sunday morning – our last
day on this job. *Richard III* this afternoon. I walked
into the theatre and there, steaming gently in the box
office, were the many people who had queued for hours
in the rain to get in to see the show. A friend of mine
was there and he'd been lining up since five o'clock this
morning. Gosh.

I chatted to a few people then pottered upstairs
to the auditorium where I was greeted by a scene of
devastation. All the stuff that has been in the last seven

25 May 2008

shows, and is not in *Richard III* this afternoon, has
been stripped away and packed into one of the many
artics lined up outside. So all the parts I've played:
Bushy, the Abbot of Westminster, Pistol, the two Dukes
of Somerset, even a dead soldier or two, are tucked
up in their little boxes, laid to rest, and will be back
in Stratford by the time Vaughan, the besuited and
bespectacled would-be murderer, has uttered his first
'Tut, tut, my lord...'

All the flying and trapeze equipment is gone. The
world retreats. And for the first time, I'm sure not for
the last, my heart has broken. Today is that day when
officially we few are to separate. We never will, of
course. But we have to say goodbye to each other. And
it is going to be hard. So much so that I think many
just won't. One by one, I'm sure we will just gradually
slip off into the ocean. That was the river, this is the
sea. And even though there is an entire estuary of tears
caught up in me, it somehow feels OK. We've been
together too long, worked too hard, been through so
much, to render 'goodbye' meaningless.

It feels like we should be given the clothes we were
wearing on that first day when we started rehearsals, a
bit of spare change, an old receipt...

As I type so the chairs in our little green room
backstage are being taken away and the notices on the
board ripped down. I have to finish.

What, of course, I have to do now is go out and
thoroughly enjoy the show. Completely be swept up one
last time by the immediacy of it all. In thought, stand
alongside those people who have stood in the rain to be
here. And who are not here too – I've already started
receiving messages from people up in Stratford saying
they wish they could be here and they are thinking

of us. This family is truly extended. It's like they're seeing us off at the airport or something, with all the possibilities and pain that brings. It's going to be one helluva ride.

Somebody's just taken the chair I was sitting on.

I feel as though my eyes and ears want to be everywhere, I don't want to miss a thing. But it'll be fun and boy, do I feel alive.

Listen. Time passes. Listen.   28 May 2008

It's three days after our final show – a final Octology which lasted from Thursday night with *Richard II*, through *Henry IV Part I & II* and *Henry V* on Friday; *Henry VI Parts I, II & III* on Saturday; and a final *Richard III* on Sunday. And I have yet to be peeled off the ceiling.

In about two weeks' time, when I realise that we're not on holiday and the absence of a pay cheque is not an administrative error, I'm sure I will have to be peeled gently off the floor, but for now I'm content to sit back and revel in the standing ovation that we had for a good seven or eight minutes on Sunday, the delight and warmth in the bar afterwards, the goodbyes and hugs, the wonderful party at Sir Christopher Bland's (the Chairman of the RSC) on Monday.

It's strange, but talking to people, I think what we all felt was going to be the high emotional point – namely, the curtain call on the final show – became relatively numbed. I certainly felt a little self-shielding at what was happening. Almost as if it was too much. It will take weeks, months, fully to be able to appreciate, enjoy and let go of this experience. But we can finally, I suppose, start thinking of a job well done. The past as well as the future. (And, until the money runs out, the present.) Maybe, just maybe, we can start to feel a little warm glow of achievement. And a thrill of excitement for what's to come.

I started working for the RSC in November 1999. On Easter Day, April 23, 2000 (Shakespeare's 436th Birthday), my father died. A week before he died I had to go back down to the Barbican and perform (and play piano) in *The Seagull*. The last thing I ever said to him as I kissed his forehead and left the room where he lay was, 'You know, I think of you every time I go on stage.' He laughed a little laugh and then said, 'Oh, I think of you every time you go on stage. Now go on. Go.' And I left and never saw him again.

A week after his funeral, I met Michael Boyd for the first time when he auditioned me to play Somerset in the first ever staging of his *Henry VI* trilogy. I must've been pretty wild-eyed, but I suppose that's fairly good for the Duke of Somerset...

Now, I grew up in Herefordshire, an hour or so away from Stratford, and my father used to take us as children to visit, and see the shows. I would revel in the theatrical images, sounds and smells, whilst my father would fill me in on what was going on. I remember my 10 year-old eyes widening at the picture of Richard Burton in its rightful place at the head of the bar in the Dirty Duck, having heard his lilting Welshness, a heritage of which my father was so proud, on a tape of *Under Milk Wood*. The words. The sounds. The words.

And I made my first resolve to be here. To live that life. Now, my father did indeed rage, rage against the dying of the light and as he passed away, so the Royal Shakespeare Company and Stratford and all it

represents have almost become a 'cradle' for me too.
As his dying and my grief have pushed me on, so I have
been working for the last two and half years on these
plays written by a man who not only mourned the death
of his father, but who in the later plays was mourning
the death of his son. So much about fathers and sons –
what they mean to each other and how their death
can affect the other. Inspiration, re-creation, wailing,
affirmation, aching loss, completion. With this job I
have been able to begin, perhaps, to understand it all.

This, of course, is just me. There is so much of
everybody else that I have been privileged to share. I
cannot even possibly begin to list here the things which
stand out in this extraordinary, amazing job. I can't,
indeed, 'begin at the beginning'. The friendships, the
work, the more work, the joy, the life, the sadness, the
arguments, the making ups, the love. A family. The
quality of the work. The collective drive and desire to do
better. To do that extra run through of the scene late at
night even though you could just go home or down the
pub. The joy of sitting backstage and hearing the shows
sing out and develop. The rush of putting on first one
play, then two, then three and so on until eventually we
had eight in our heads and up and running. We used
to say, in the height of summer during the Complete
Works Festival 2006, when we were putting on three
shows and working 13-hour days, 'Blimey, what's it going
to be like when we do all eight?!'

Well, now we know and it was unlike any other
show we will ever do again. There really will be nothing
like it.

We played. At times, I was that wide-eyed innocent
10 year-old boy at play again. And I cannot believe that
it's over.

The truth is, of course, it never will be. Not in the minds of the many cast, crew and creative team; and those who saw and loved it. I DID think of my old man every time I was about to do my first entrance of each play. And I could feel him thinking of me. Through me or not, he was there. During this job I have finally been able to walk free from the shadow of his untimely death. I was safe within the bosom of a truly great group of people and from within that could let go. Perform. Live.

A couple of weeks ago, staying in the flat overlooking The Roundhouse where I lived for three years from 1999 to 2002, I wrote down on a scrap of paper: 'Living in a flat where I lived when Dad died; working – on a show I first started a week after he died – in a ROUNDhouse; things have come full circle. TIME to move on!'

But if the death of my father and these shows – the experience AND Shakespeare – have shown me anything, it is that one life, one moment in time, be it theatrical or not, or however ephemeral, can last forever. As long as we remember. Then, we can let it go. And that is history. In these History Plays we have found history and play. And I hope that is our future too.

Time and History are cyclical and linear together. We are all at the threshold point of our own play.

'Listen. Time passes. Listen.' As Dylan Thomas wrote in *Under Milk Wood*.

And as Shakespeare wrote:

'Small time, but in that small, most greatly lived' – this wonderful, wonder-filled 'job'.

Thank you. Good night.

RESPONSES

WHAT *fun to hear about* Richard II *straight from the Bushy's mouth! Now we the* Histories *fans are eagerly awaiting a similar account of the progress of the two* Henries. *Having seen the first preview of* Richard II *two weeks ago and been completely sucked into its fascinating politics-as-choreography universe, so different from that of the previous tetralogy, it'll be very interesting to revisit it when I come back in mid August to see it again, plus the* Henries. *Looking forward to that immensely, but in the meantime, 'Blog on, blog on, the footpath way', as the Bard (almost) put it.*

Best regards,

Kiki

LOVE *the blog – I already feel part of the* Histories *project having been an addict since seeing the* Henry VI *trilogy for the first time a year ago. Changed the rest of last year for me – I came up to Stratford to see you guys do it again and again, and forced all my friends to go too. Revelation for all of us.* Richard III *just as thrilling, and we've already been to see* Richard II *– and in honour of our trilogy addiction of last year, a few of us are going on a pilgrimage to see you do the new 'trilogy' for the first time next Thursday. Anyway, discovering the blog is a real buzz – great to feel even more a part of such an amazing project than we already do as devoted audience members. Thanks Nick and good luck with the bottle scene in the future...sounds dangerous you poor sod.*

Cheers,

Anna

WE *saw the performances on 29 December, and they were enthralling performances – definitely added to our family list of great theatre expe-*

riences. We thought Henry V *with its exciting battle scenes was a great finish to our history play series, well worth a standing ovation (though you probably didn't spot us standing up in the back row!).*

Rosy

. . . .

I was looking at the website after spending a truly wonderful weekend living the lives of Richard II *through to* Henry V *and as a bonus meeting a few of you in the Mucky Duck on Saturday night and even buying a couple of you a drink – Few; too bloody few I might add – as every last one of that astonishing ensemble deserved a drink on us at least.*

Anyway, I digress! I wanted to say what a magnificent and life enhancing experience the Histories have been – I think my sister and I will be feeding off it for a long time to come and are busy trying to fit in another stab (forgive the pun) at the Henry VI *trilogy before all finishes and trying to persuade our menfolk that they might enjoy it too!*

Please pass on a huge and heartfelt thank you to everyone involved for a magical culmination to all that has gone before.

Jane

. . . .

IT'S so much fun to read your blog and find out a bit more about what is going on behind (and under) the scenes.

My husband and I found out about The Complete Works when we ended up in Stratford-upon-Avon totally by accident in July 2006 after a hiking holiday gone wrong. It was then when we first saw Henry VI Part I. *We didn't know the play and first didn't want to go (unknown, unloved, you know), but since the tickets were cheaper, it being only the 2nd performance, we decided to go after all. And we were totally swept off our feet! We absolutely loved the wonderful acting, the fighting scenes, the costumes, the language and also the courtyard theatre in itself! So much that we came back the following evening to see the same play again. And we came back the following months to see every other play of the Histories Cycle.*

We have grown so fond of these plays and of its actors that we booked tickets for the 8 History plays on the weekend of 6–9 March 2008 to enjoy them all once again.

Many thanks to the actors, directors and everyone involved in these performances!

We are already counting down the days until 6 March!

Hilde

• •

DEAR Nick, and all – I have just arrived home after watching all eight of the plays this weekend, and knew that somehow, I had to say thank you to you all. I'm sure you must get thousands of emails like this, but nevertheless, this is one of the most heartfelt thanks.

I have been brought up on Shakespeare and the theatre, and was lucky enough to graduate from Warwick University last year, and so was able to see a good dose of The Complete Works, although previous to this weekend, I had only seen Richard III *from your ensemble. But nothing I have ever seen before lives up to the cycle of plays you all presented over the weekend; there was not a weak link, not a moment that didn't make the adrenaline race and the heart pound, and I have never before felt tears in my eyes at the final blackout, simply because the experience was over.*

You all worked so hard, and yet it seemed so effortless, so natural; you seemed to live the parts, and most importantly, love them, and love performing, and that is infectious, and helped to elevate the already impossibly high standard of work that you were presenting.

I could go on forever with all the individual things that I loved about the weekend, however the whole ensemble was fabulous, and everyone worked so hard, and had such wonderful talent. You all appeared to work together seamlessly, everything and everyone was a real joy to watch.

Please pass on my thanks to everyone involved in the production if it is at all possible, and I'd like to say again, this has been an experience that I shall never forget.

Thank you,

Hannah

DEAR Nick, *I have just come home from Stratford-upon-Avon after having lived for four days in and around the Courtyard Theatre watching the eight History Plays on March 6–9th. Looking forward to it, I realised I might get an indigestion of it after a few plays. How wrong was I! It was absolutely overwhelming! I loved every second of every play! I loved the acting, the staging, the language, the costumes, the music and sound effects, the Courtyard Theatre and the whole atmosphere during these eight plays. I feel like having lived in another world for four days and now being dropped off in everyday life again.*

I think it is such an amazing achievement by all the actors to remember all their lines and to create tension or emotion, or be genuinely funny in every play again, as if it was for the first time every time again. It was such an intense experience, I will never forget it!

Yours sincerely,

Hilde

I was worried that the blog would have finished after the Histories quit Stratford, but I'd largely forgotten the London run. It's wonderful to be able to keep the whole experience fresh in my mind a little longer!

As someone who was lucky enough to be at the Glorious Moment in its glorious entirety, I can't heap enough praise on everyone involved. Mainly the cast, obviously, but with the amount of technical wizardry involved, the crew must have been run off their feet. There was never as much as a technical hiccup that I noticed in the 8 performances, which speaks volumes. (I was honestly surprised – staggered, in fact – by the smallness of the crew when they came to take their bow after Richard III. I was expecting legions.)

During the official reception after the last show I was lucky enough to be able to talk to a fair few of the cast, some at length, and the sense that it'd been a mutual experience came up again and again. It was genuinely one of the most extraordinary experiences of my life, and now I'm just waiting for my first opportunity to say 'I was there' with regard to it.

The curtain may come down for the last time in May, but if I'm in any way a representative sample, these Histories will not be forgotten any time soon. Bravo. To everybody, bravo.

Myfanwy

PS Any plans to put all these blogs together in a book?? They've been very enjoyable and made me feel a little bit a part of the amazing 'Histories' (as well as making me want even more to give up my day job and go begging for backstage work at the RSC!).

- -

I saw the 'Staging History' weekend in Stratford. It was hard enough leaving after four days and returning to normal life – I can't imagine how you are all feeling. Now you have only the two complete runs left I

guessed it was time to say how much I loved the shows, so THANK YOU.
They truly were glorious moments I hope never to forget.

Best wishes to all of you – I'll be looking out for you all on future cast
lists!

Emma

· ·

WELL, hallelujah, I just found your blogs, through fiddling about online.
I was in the audience for the Glorious Moment and wasn't it fantastic? It
rates up there as one of the best few days of my life.

I was truly moved and uplifted by all the performances and had a real
sense of loss at the end...standing in the hotel car park on the Sunday
evening howling and crying because I didn't want it to end...and if I felt
like that, how must you all have felt leaving Stratford and ultimately
giving your last performances at the Roundhouse.

I'm a sucker for the plays, for the whole movement of the ensemble,
the extra life you create in your having been together and evolving. I'm
thrilled to see all the fantastic and well deserved reviews of the transfer
to the Roundhouse. Michael Billington in the Guardian *loved them, and*
rightly said that it will remain in the memory of those that attended as
a golden moment. Never underestimate the pleasure you have given so
many and the inspiration that has fired those who witnessed the plays.
The Guardian *editor said this week that someone should step in and*
film them before they are lost forever – I wish it would happen.

Please continue blogging. Tell us what the final 2 weeks were like. Where
will you all go? I wish you and your fellow actors every success in finding
more work...

Written several days later...well I had the most fabulous day on your last
Friday of performances – if anything they were more vibrant than the
Glorious Moment. I sat on the Terrace between performances soaking up

every last minute of the plays and of the energy of the Ensemble. Needless to say, thank you to you and your colleagues. You were all brilliant.

Kate

. . . .

BANK Holiday Saturday lunch time:

We are currently in between Henry VI Parts I and II of the final octology of the run. So far the plays have been fantastic. I have seen all the plays over the last 2 years at Stratford, but wanted to see them all in historical order for one last time. It has been fascinating to see how the plays have changed, grown and adapted over that 2 year period. The performers are to be commended for their dedication, ability and hard work. It is just a shame that there will be no permanent record of this achievement, except in the memories of the performers and those people lucky and sensible enough to have bought tickets and seen the plays. Good luck for the last 3 plays, I know they are going to live up to my expectations.

I have also been reading these blogs over the 2 year period and have thoroughly enjoyed the extra depth they have given to the plays and the process that this great undertaking has undergone.

Jenny

. . . .

HELLO Nick (and RSC people)

I guess it must all be over now, please could you blog again and let us all know how it ended and what everyone is up to next.

I saw the whole cycle in Stratford and was utterly moved, if I had the time and money I would have come to see every play again in London. Unfortunately the closest that I could get was to read your blog.

I hope the audience on the last night gave you the standing ovation that you all deserve, and wish the cast and crew the best for the future, if I was a casting director I would hire every single one of you.

Zoe

. . . .

SUCH a beautiful read, Nick – and eerie too, that you've come to the same conclusion about the Histories cycle that myself and a fellow addict from your wide-eyed audience arrived at when we caught up for a debrief about the experience over the weekend. We'd both long, long been dreading the end and I thought I'd be a wreck at that final curtain call last Sunday. In fact, the hugeness of the moment seemed not quite to hit – it was thrilling and I did get teary-eyed, but it was not the full-on punch of loss that I'd been steeling myself for, and dreading. For a couple of days I thought 'Oh, I'm just in denial – it'll hit soon'. But it hasn't and that I believe is because something this loved does not end, and my subconscious must have realised this. The fellow addict has had the same feeling all week. As you say (and you put it so perfectly) one moment in time can last forever, as long as we remember. And so this glorious moment will always be with us. A good lesson for life.

Great good luck with whatever you do next – there are a lot of us eager to go and see whatever anyone in the whole Histories company does in the future. Just to top up those precious memories, and to create new ones.

Eleanor

. . . .

THANK you for producing these last three blog entries – I couldn't believe you would leave us waiting for an ending and not produce one. Ending well is the first step in grieving for something and grieve you all will, for the ensemble, the mission, the plays.

I shared in the moment with just 12 of your performances, but find that I mourn the passing of them, never to be repeated, never re-experienced. Perhaps as you say, they continue if we remember them and I do regularly. I re-read the plays and look at programmes and remember an idyllic lunch on the Roundhouse Terrace in the sun, watching you all laughing. I enjoyed seeing that interaction as much as that of your characters on stage.

A final well done and good luck in your future ventures. It is impossible to put into words the joy you have conveyed in these performances. For some of your audience, sharing this magic was life changing.

Kate

PHOTOGRAPHS

Key to photographers

EK: *Ellie Kurttz*

RD: *Robert Day*

LB: *Lucy Barriball*

SH: *Stewart Hemley*

RW: *Roger Watkins*

KB: *Keith Bartlett*

Opposite: Meet the family. The Histories Ensemble in The Courtyard, Stratford-upon-Avon. Cast, Crew and 'Creatives'. (RD)

Eight plays, 34 actors, 264 parts, 210,000 words, 1389 minutes (just under 24 hours), 4 bucketfuls of sand, 100 tennis balls, 120 weapons, 30 guns, 15 litres of blood, just over 800 costumes, 80 costume rails, 8 loads of washing, 30 props and costume skips, and 40 wigs. And a whole lotta love.

The set on its 'thrust' stage in The Courtyard Theatre. The audience were lit just as much as the actors on stage. The chairs are for a scene in *Richard III*. They were the only bits of 'furniture' – along with a couple of metal beds, an old armchair for Falstaff, a rusty metal box (which doubled as a throne) and a moving staircase – that we used in the whole eight plays. Ropes and ladders did the rest. [LB]

Richard II, Act 1 sc 1. The beginning of twenty-four hours of theatre… The ghost of the murdered Duke of Gloucester lies in the middle of Richard's court as Bolingbroke (Clive Wood, *left*) and Mowbray (John Mackay, *right*) challenge each other over his death. [EK]

Henry VI Part III. Paul Hamilton (*left*) and Self (*right*) as the Earl of Oxford and Young Duke of Somerset after the final Lancastrian defeat at the Battle of Tewkesbury. Katy Stephens (*centre*), as Margaret their leader, hooded, is dragged on by Keith Dunphy from the 'Hell Mouth'. [EK]

The coronation of Richard III. Jonathan Slinger (*left*) as Richard, and Hannah Barrie (*right*) as Lady Anne, prepare to walk up the steps to be crowned by the ghost of Richard's father, the Duke of York (Clive Wood, *centre*). Before them lies the prostrate ghost of Henry VI (Chuk Iwuji). [EK]

Right: Rehearsing the Jack Cade sequences in Clapham, with John Mackay's head fearfully close to the ceiling (see page 21). [EK]

Above left: Terry King, Fight Director. 'Aaaaand… Badumph!' [EK]

Above right: In rehearsal. Jonathan Slinger as the young Richard in *Henry VI Part III* being restrained in the Parley before Towton. [EK]

In rehearsal. (*L to R*) Chuk Iwuji, Roger Watkins, Katy Stephens, Lex Shrapnel and Kieran Hill. The reaction to young Richard's behaviour in the Parley before Towton. [EK]

Above left: Michael Boyd, a bit of a genius. There's quite a lot going on in that head. [EK]

Above right: Self, receiving a note from Michael. Am I going to use the machete on him? [EK]

Above left: Richard II (Jon Slinger, *left*) bids goodbye to Bolingbroke (Clive Wood, *right*) before the fight with Mowbray in Act 1 sc 3. Bushy (Self) and Queen Isabel (Hannah Barrie) look on. I'm there to catch her if she falls off the stairs in that dress. [EK]

Above right: Sand was poured down on Richard II as a motif for his downfall, and a metaphor for how his own people threw dust on him after being usurped by Bolingbroke. Here, the Ghost of Richard II appears to Bolingbroke, now Henry IV, amidst his sandy cloud. That sand got everywhere. [EK]

Above left: Father and son. Clive Wood (*left*) as the dying Henry IV, and Geoffrey Streatfeild (*right*) as Prince Hal, having taken the crown a little prematurely. [EK]

Above right: Henry V (Geoffrey Streatfeild) and Katherine (Alexia Healy) unite England and France. Yeah, right… [EK]

Henry VI Part I. The English in ceremonial robes at the coronation of Henry VI in Paris. From left to right: Patrice Naiambana, Chuk Iwuji, Geoffrey Streatfeild, Julius D'Silva, and Clive Wood. [EK]

Above left: Henry VI Part III. The future Richard III arrives through the 'Hell Mouth' to murder the imprisoned Henry VI. That metal box was his throne two plays earlier... [EK]

Above right: The dream sequence in *Richard III.* The Ghost of Henry VI approaches the Earl of Richmond (Lex Shrapnel) to encourage him in the next day's battle. The naked and exposed Richard III, whose dream this is, looks on. [EK]

The Pavanne 'Blob' in *Richard II*. The opening image of the 'Octology'. [EK]

Hal (Geoffrey Streatfeild, *left*) and Falstaff (David Warner, *right*) in their first scene in *Henry IV Part I*. [EK]

Hal (Streatfeild) bites the jugular of Hotspur (Lex Shrapnel) to finally kill him in their climactic battle at the end of *Henry IV Part I*. Lovely. Falstaff (Warner) lies behind, feigning death. [EK]

Above left: John Mackay on his trapeze as the Dauphin in *Henry V*. [EK]

Top right: Henry V. Self as Pistol being force-fed a leek by Jon Slinger as Fluellen. I spent nearly a year reeking of the things. [EK]

Bottom right: Henry V cradling the dead Boy (Wela Frasier), who in our production had been with him as Peto all the way from *Henry IV Part I* in the Tavern scenes. [EK]

Above left: Henry VI Part I. Clive Wood (*left*) as Richard Plantagenet and Self (*right*) as the Duke of Somerset square up in The Temple Garden scene. Note the cage with all the roses. (It was cut after this performance – see page 32.) [EK]

Above right: Self with finger, modelling leather trousers and fur cloak. A thousand ocelots died in the making of that cloak. Only joking. [EK]

Above left: Henry VI Part I. (*R to L*) Katy Stephens, Ann Ogbomo, Hannah Barrie and Alexia Healy as Joan of Arc and her 'fiends' about to whip Lord Talbot's hide in a sword fight. 'Christ's mother helps me, else I were too weak.' [EK]

Above right: Henry VI Part I. Katy Stephens, as Joan of Arc, curses and screams as she is burnt. Moments later she would appear from the 'Hell Mouth' as the newly-minted Margaret, looking like Gloria Swanson. I still don't know how she did it so quickly. [EK]

Above left: Henry VI Part I. Lex Shrapnel as Young John Talbot, lifeless and bloodied, is held aloft on slings after the 'Blob', and Keith Bartlett as the fatally wounded Talbot is left to lament his son's death. (See page 22.) [EK]

Above right: Henry VI Part II. Hannah Barrie, as the witch Margery Jourdain, is hoisted from the ground and pulls from it the Ghosts of the dead Talbots, echoing their own deaths. Later they would come back to kill the Duke of Suffolk on their Styx-like boat and take part in Jack Cade's rebellion. [EK]

Above left: Henry VI Part I. Self, as Salisbury, being blown off a ladder and getting head covered in blood. Fun. [EK]

Above right: Dying self on ladder. About to get lifted back up to the gods not knowing which way is up. [EK]

Below: Jack Cade (John Mackay) swings on his trapeze above his motley assortment of rebels, ghosts and butchers. Note the dead pig on the tower. [EK]

Left: Henry VI Part III. As the final Battle of Tewkesbury rages offstage, filling the theatre with a cacophony of drums, Chuk Iwuji as Henry VI is caught in a lonely cascade of red and white feathers. [EK]

Below: Henry VI Part III. Having stabbed Henry VI to death, Richard of Gloucester rages at the world over his body, while Henry seeps blood all over the stage. There were two guys manhandling a pump directly underneath Chuk as the blood flowed out from under him. [EK]

Above left: Richard III's own particular brand of wooing Hannah Barrie as Lady Anne. The birthmark symbolises the blood shed by all Jonathan Slinger's previous characters in the 'Octology'. [EK]

Above right: Richard III. Just when you thought it was safe, Henry VI's widow Margaret (Katy Stephens) returns to the English court with the bones of her son whom they had killed. [EK]

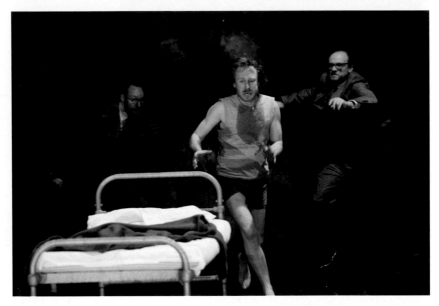

Above: Keith Dunphy (*left*) and Self (*right*) make various bespectacled attempts to kill the Duke of Clarence (Jimmy Tucker, *centre*). [EK]

The Curtain Call at the end of 'The Glorious Moment' in The Courtyard Theatre. [SH]

The Courtyard in all its glory at the Curtain Call for *Henry IV Part I*, acknowledging the musicians. [SH]

Top left: Richard II. Green (Anthony Shuster, *left*) and Bushy (Self) receive their death sentence from Bolingbroke (Clive Wood, *right*). I'm delighted by it, obviously. [RW]

Top right: Henry V. The dying French at Agincourt. [RW]

Above left: Henry VI Part II. Holland and Bevis (Forbes Masson, *left*, and Jon Slinger, *right*) enter with the body of Suffolk freshly separated from its head to herald the Jack Cade rebellion. Suffolk was killed on a boat hence the fish heads. Honest. [RW]

Above right: Henry V. Self slapping Fluellen (Slinger, *left*). [RW]

Below: Jon Slinger as the Ghost of Richard II plays table tennis with Luke Neal in the foyer of The Courtyard. Once you've died, you're usually better for some reason… [KB]

EPILOGUE

WHILST cooking in the kitchen last week I had *University Challenge* on in the background, so that with every impossible question I could never hope to answer, I could crush another clove of garlic. Suddenly the knife slid from my hand as I heard Jeremy Paxman ask the question: '"It combines the scope of *War and Peace*, *The Sopranos* and the Bible" – to what was the Artistic Director of the RSC, Michael Boyd, referring – an event which took place in London in April and May of 2008?'

It was a starter question. Ten points.

Nobody got it.

'No?' said Jeremy, 'It was Shakespeare's History Plays. Right, another starter…'

Not only did I finally know the answer to a question, but I'd actually been IN the question, in a roundabout way. It was another unique little feeling to add to the many emotions ranging from pride to pain I have felt over the six months since we finished The Histories.

As far as I can see, it is already becoming an iconic show in theatre, ranging from being a question on a TV quiz (surely that is the height of iconic status?), to many of us being stopped on the street in London, of all places, to be told how much people had enjoyed The Histories. They never stop you on the street in London normally. The Head of Casting at the RSC, Hannah Miller, told me the other day how Drama School leavers are queuing up to try to join the company, as they saw the shows and it inspired them to keep going with their training.

Although maybe that's all just in our minds, us actors, as we press on with getting on. It's inevitable that there is some crystallising of the memories to make them shine with a little more lustre. But one of the beauties of having kept a blog is that it did occasionally manage to catch a glimpse, a moment, of what is was we were going through and is therefore sealed in time, like a stag's head on a wall.

But we move on. I shot an episode of *Heartbeat*, playing a Polish pianist returning to find his lost wartime girlfriend. I spent a week practising the piano for 6 hours a day and very little time on the accent. So what you'll get is 10 seconds of me playing the piano and the rest of the hour with me sounding like Arnold Schwarzenegger. 250,000 people saw The Histories. 5 million will see that.

Jon Slinger and Geoffrey Streatfeild were cast in a police drama mini-series. So you've got Richard III and Henry V wandering around a police station. Which makes me laugh. Apparently, they found some table tennis bats and balls on set, and started playing on their desk. The set carpenters whisked them up a proper table, with police tape for a net, and they were off. Others started playing and began to comment on how good Geoff and Jon were and asked if they'd been practising. 'About two and a half years, every day' was the reply as they fired another backhand winner past the bemused opposition.

Lex got cast in *Minder*, and Clive played a baddie in it for an episode. John Mackay and Julius were both down at Chichester for a while, and now Julius is playing Mr Bumble in *Oliver!* in the West End. Alexia did an episode of *The Bill*, Hannah did the *Casualty* Christmas Special. Luke did *Midsomer Murders*, Chuk did a film. Forbes is doing Pete Postlethwaite's *Lear* in Liverpool. Matt, rather aptly, did *Monkey* at the West Yorkshire Playhouse. The list goes on.

There have been disappointments. We didn't go to America – which we should have done. We didn't all get cast in the next big BBC costume drama, or, indeed, the next big ensemble – at the RSC or anywhere else. I remember doing a Question & Answer session with Alexia and Geoffrey for the 'Friends of the RSC', in our last week at The Round-house. The question was asked for all of us, 'What next for you after this?' Alexia replied in all truthfulness that she'd got a job lined up as a waitress in a bar and to a person the whole audience started laughing. They thought it was a joke. It wasn't.

Life as an actor is tough and it's getting tougher. The good times are very good. The bad times are very bad. When you've been out of the race for three years it's a hard ride. And whilst, for me, the money has run out and the rollercoaster has dipped below ground for a little while, I'm still on it. Still holding on to the bar with all the joy I can muster, screaming.

And hopefully I'm still open. Someone asked me the other day what I thought the legacy of The Histories would be. I really have no idea – that is for others to decide. We won a couple of awards. Which is nice. But if I had a choice it would be that the openness with which we played – cast, crew and creative team alike – is continued in the nature of ensemble. Over the course of two and a half years we became open to each other and the audience. I hope that generosity will continue within the the RSC and I'm sure it will. There is a mountain still to be climbed, new and higher summits to conquer.

Theatre exists in a moment, stories last forever.

Meanwhile, any job I get, I shall attack with a vigour I never thought possible and that is the professional legacy it leaves for me.

And that can't be bad.

Personally, as I stand chopping the garlic in my kitchen – after six months the novelty of cooking still hasn't worn off – and listening to questions about us on the telly and hearing that we've won an award, I feel a huge and tangible sense of pride in all that we achieved.

But the most important thing is, those people that I met over the course of two and a half years are all still my friends and will be forever.

Wherever we are, we are one big, silly, loving, dysfunctional family. We few, we happy few.

And in that, above all things, I'm the luckiest person alive.

> 'Old men forget yet all shall be forgot
>   But he'll remember with advantages
>   What feats he did that day…
>   We few, we happy few, we band of brothers'.

NA
November 2008

WHO'S WHO OF THE HISTORIES

There are over 700 people who work for the the Royal Shakespeare Company, all of whom work extremely hard to bring the shows to an audience. It would be impossible here to list everyone involved with the project, but the following is an attempt by me to include everyone who was part of 'The Histories Ensemble' in the most immediate fashion: all of those people who at the end of the special 'Glorious Moments' of eight shows in four days emerged blinking into the lights, all dressed in black, and took a deserved bow with the rest of the cast. Every one of them had a direct bearing on the show. As for all the Green Room, Box Office, RSC Café, Shop and Front of House Staff who all had to put up with us thundering past them, sword in hand and covered in blood, we lived and worked with them on such a daily basis they were just as much a part of 'The Ensemble' as any actor or director. Without them, the shows would not have been what they were. They are the life of The Courtyard and The Roundhouse.

The Actors (in alphabetical order):

Nicholas Asbury

Keith Bartlett

Antony Bunsee

Richard Cordery

Julius D'Silva

Wela Frasier

Paul Hamilton

Kieran Hill

Chuk Iwuji

Forbes Masson

Patrice Naiambana

Sandy Neilson

Miles Richardson

Anthony Shuster

Katy Stephens

James Tucker

Roger Watkins

Hannah Barrie

Maureen Beattie

Rob Carroll

Matt Costain

Keith Dunphy

Geoffrey Freshwater

Alexia Healy

Tom Hodgkins

John Mackay

Chris McGill

Luke Neal

Ann Ogbomo

Lex Shrapnel

Jonathan Slinger

Geoffrey Streatfeild

David Warner

Clive Wood

Michael Boyd: Artistic Director of the Royal Shakespeare Company and Director of seven of the eight plays

Richard Twyman: Associate Director; Director on *Henry IV Part II*

Donnacadh O'Briain: Assistant Director

Denise Wood: Producer

Tom Piper: Chief Associate Designer of the RSC and Set and Costume Design on The Histories

Emma Williams: Costume Design & Costume Supervisor

Liz Ranken: Movement

Andrea J Cox: Sound Designer

Terry King: Fight Director

Matt Costain: Director of Rope Work

Alison Bomber: Company Voice Work

Poppy Hall: Costume Supervisor

Heather Carson: Lighting Designer

Mark Graham: Production Manager

Stage Management: **Michael Dembowicz, Zoe Donegan, Robbie Cullen, Erin Murphy, Fran O'Donnell, Juliette Taylor**

Music: **James Jones, John Woolf, Kevin Pitt, Edward Watson, Sianed Jones**

Assistants to Michael Boyd: **Thea Jones, Liza Frank**

Casting Directors: **Ginny Schiller, Sam Jones**

Wigs & Make-Up: **Laura Odom, Charlotte Griffiths, Fiona Matthews, Rachel Seal, Sandra Smith, Fiona Keston, Jo-Anne Tuplin, Jennifer Simons, Kimberley Boyce**

Wardrobe: **Carolyn Daniels, Liz McCartney, Jennifer Binns, Marion Harrison, Claire Louise Hardie, Yvonne Gilbert, Helena Rose, Dawn Coulson, Linda Williams, Michael Nolan, Linda Hood, Michelle Davis, Joise Horton Josefa Adlem, Joanne Wollington, Claire Arden, Anita Oram, Rachael Halliwell, Natasha Blumson, Leanne Angus, Michelle Davies, Paula McIntosh, Miwa Mitsuhashi, Rachel Farrimond**

Stage Staff: **Matt Aston, Dom Chen, Tom Horton, Steve Keeley, Simon Packer, Tom Watts, Kevin Wimperis, Darren Guy, Roger Haymes, Al Pitts, Mark Collins, Tom Mellon, Grant Skidmore,**

Dave Hill, Dave Lawson Terry Bennett, Ben O'Grady, James Stuart, Max Brown, James Mitchell, Craig Almond, Robert Weatherhead, Lucy Thorpe

Automation: **Richard Sharp, Ian MacDonald, Becky Hardwicke, Rich Storry Eric Dixon, Andy Marshall, Darren Williams**

Lighting: **Al West, Trevor Wallace, Simon Spencer, Jake Brain, Kevin Carson, Dave Richardson, Craig Sheppard, Lauren Watson, Matt Peel, Dan Tilley, Vince Herbert, Simon Bayliss, Keith Cookson, Caroline Burrell, Jonathan Ruddick, Alex Mannix**

Sound: **Mike Compton, Tim Oliver, Tim McCormick, Simon Moloney, Chris Vernon, Andy Franks, Sarah Hollyman, Ed Borgnis, Chris Vernon, Jeremy Dunn**

Ariel equipment & installation **(They got us in the air!)**: **Joe Hull of High Performance Rigging & Steve Robinson**

RSC Roundhouse Technical Manager: **Julian Cree**

RSC Roundhouse Production Electrician: **Phil Supple**

RSC Roundhouse Back of House: **David Tanquerqay**

RSC Roundhouse Seating: **David Harraway**

RSC Roundhouse Logistics: **Gareth Baston**

They all worked very hard, and it was a very big party at the end.

The Histories Awards List

TMA Awards 2008: **Michael Boyd** Best Director

Whatsonstage Theatregoer's Choice Awards 2009:
　　Katy Stephens Best Actress
　　Best Shakespearean Production

Playshakespeare.com Falstaff Awards:
　　Heather Carson Best Lighting Design
　　Terry King Best Choreography/Fight Director

Evening Standard Awards 2008: **Special Editor's Award**

Olivier Awards 2009:
　　Best Company Performance
　　Best Revival
　　Best Costume Design

GLOSSARY

The world of theatre can be a strange world of technical jargon and age old shorthand which can render any outsider dumbfounded. Throughout the text I have tried to be as explanatory as I could; however, here is a brief glossary of terms, sayings and stories that may prove useful...

Acting ASM

Acting Assistant Stage Manager. Becoming less and less prevalent, it is used to describe the job of one of the lowliest people in the theatre. An actor fresh out of drama school, with no experience, or in the days of **Rep** (see below), someone who even wandered in off the street and wanted to go on the stage, was given this job and would have to make the tea, sweep the floor – all manner of things, but in turn might occasionally be allowed to go on stage and say a line or two, or understudy a part. Some of the greatest actors of the last 100 years were Acting ASMs – and the Stage Management team these days always say you can spot the actors who have been one, as they always return their props to the right place and generally consider the Stage Management team to be something more than servants.

Agents

Most actors have agents who are supposed to find work, negotiate contracts and generally manage an actor's career. They take anything from 10 to 20 per cent of your income, depending on the type of job.

Aggregation

As in 'Separation, Liminality and Aggregation'. See pages 92–3.

Artistic Director

The head of a Theatre Company or Theatre, who, as well as directing plays, dictates the Artistic Policy of the organisation. A figurehead and a leader.

Automation

The new technical way of 'flying', with steel wires and winches driven by computers and weight ratios. Ultra modern and safer than a beefy bloke, who's usually been down the pub for a couple of sharpeners before the show, clutching on to the other end of the rope as you dangle above the audience.

Barbican

The massive arts complex in the City of London, the main theatre of which was used as the RSC's London home from 1982 to 2002.

Battle of Barnet

A battle in *Henry VI Part 3* Act 5 sc 1. The Earl of Warwick, who fought to put the Duke of York on the throne, switched sides to the Lancastrian King, Henry VI, because of the behaviour of York's son, crowned as Edward IV, when made king. In this battle he is slain by Edward himself and the 'Yorkists' finally have the upper hand in the the Wars of the Roses.

Begin at the beginning
The opening of Dylan Thomas' play *Under Milk Wood* (1953):
'To begin at the beginning. It is Spring, moonless night in the small town, starless and bible black...'

Blob
See pages 21–2.

'Blow winds and Crack your Cheeks'
William Shakespeare. *King Lear* Act 3 sc 2.

Broadsword
A massive sword held with two hands which preceded the thinner and lighter rapier sword.

Bushy
Sir John Bushy, an acolyte and staunch supporter of Richard II. In Shakespeare's play he forms part of a triumvirate that flatters the King and are described by Bolingbroke as 'Bushy, Bagot and Green / The Caterpillars of the Commonwealth'

Cade, Jack
A Kentish man who in *Henry VI Part II* is coerced by Richard Plantagenet, Duke of York, to stage a rebellion against the King, Henry VI.

Calls
The word 'Call' has become a generic term in theatre for the rehearsal times and show time. You can have a Fight or Dance 'Call'. A rehearsal 'call' for the next day. A show Call. 'What time is my call tomorrow' is a familiar cry of any actor reaching for their last pint in the pub...

Dauphin
The eldest son of the King of France. He makes an appearance in *Henry V* and *Henry VI Part I*. Very often called the Dolphin by the French-hating English.

Duck
The Dirty Duck, a pub on Waterside, Stratford-upon-Avon, which was originally called The Black Swan. It's slap bang in the middle of all the theatres and has been an 'actors'' pub for generations. (See Page 27.)

Ensemble
In this context, a group of theatre makers, from actors through to directors and stage management that work together over a long period of time.

Eccles
A character played by Spike Milligan in *The Goon Show*, a comedy radio show of the 1950s, with lots of guttural sounds and glottle stops.

Fight Captain

A lot of shows have different disciplines which need to be rehearsed almost every day. Various actors, whether it's because they're good at it or are simply good at bossing their peers around, are appointed Captains of those disciplines to oversee the practice at 'Calls' (see above) before the show. I was Fight Captain, but you can have a Dance Captain, Singing Captain, etc.

Fly

When an actor, or piece of set, is suspended in any way in mid-air.

Flies

The area above the stage where all the paraphernalia of flying is kept. Ropes, scenery, ladders. In most older theatres you will see a tower above the stage so that massive bits of scenery, or pieces of canvas with a scene painted on them – flats – could be lowered into the stage way down below. Understandably, it's a very restricted area – and usually very dangerous. Hence 'Flymen' are a breed on their own... In earlier days of theatre, many of these flymen would be sailors as they were accustomed to lots of ropes and tackle and being up on high. They would communicate to each other by using the whistles of the navy world, so any actor pottering onto stage, tunelessly whistling to himself, might get a load of scenery flattening him. Hence, it is still considered bad luck to whistle on stage.

Fourth Wall

In a 'proscenium arch' theatre the stage is surrounded by three walls and the audience look at them from the auditorium. By bringing the stage into the audience more, that 'fourth wall' is broken and the audience become more included in the show.

Gods

An expression for the highest parts of a theatre, whether it be the top row of the audience, or way up in the **Flies**.

Globe Theatre

Shakespeare's Globe Theatre built on the South Bank, in the 1990s, very near to the original site of The Globe Theatre that Shakespeare and his contempories built in 1599. It sticks to the Elizabethan design and is open to the elements. It's wonderful.

Harfleur

The battle in *Henry V*, Act 3 sc 2, where Henry opens with the line: 'Once more unto the breach, dear friends, once more'.

Iambics

For most of his work, Shakespeare wrote in verse. This has a meter, or beat to it, and is one of the hardest and most contentious things to get right as a Shakespearean actor. It is called Iambic Pentameter, in the sense that there are FIVE beats to the line: de-DUM, de-DUM, de-DUM, de-DUM, de-DUM. Or, for example: 'Once MORE unTO the BREECH dear FRIENDS once MORE', or 'A HORSE a HORSE, my KINGdom FOR a HORSE'. That's the theory, at least. It is certainly true, in my experience, that if you are stuck on a line – what it means; how it is coming across etc – if you go back to just sticking with the meter, the rhythm, it's a fair bet it works. The old man knew what he was doing.

Lancastrians
The side fighting for the King, Henry VI, who was also Duke of Lancaster. They had a red rose for an emblem.

Listen. Time passes. Listen.
Under Milk Wood, Dylan Thomas (1953)

Lighting Grid
A series of bars in the roof of the theatre, very often forming a grid pattern, which form the base upon which lights can be hung at different places for a show.

Lights (green and red)
Most theatres have a series of 'cue lights' backstage. Tiny little electric boxes which flash red for 'stand by' – meaning that a cue is about to come up – and green for 'go'. These are operated by the Deputy Stage Manager (DSM) whose job it is to 'run', or cue, the show. It's one of the most important, and tricky, jobs in theatre. They have a board in front them with a whole series of red and green lights which they operate with the skill of an organist. A good DSM will often dictate how the show is paced, how it will flow for the audience, and can be as much an artistic job as it is technical. They sit in on every rehearsal, and their communication with the Director is an important fulcrum around which any show swings. They also have the script in front of them and can remind any actor if they are beginning to skip some lines…

When were doing *Henry V*, for example, there were about 12 of us crammed underneath the stage in pitch blackness, all under different traps and not able to hear a thing. All we could focus on was the little red light, and then, at the green, we would all emerge, blinking, out of the traps at the same time. At least, that was the idea…

Liminality
As in 'Separation, Liminality and Aggregation'. See pages 92–3.

'Method'
A style of acting pioneered in the 1930s and '40s at the Actor's Studio in New York by many American film actors under the tutelage of Lee Strasberg, being heavily influenced by the work of Stanislavksy and Chekhov, and very often missing their point. Total immersion in the emotions of the character is needed in order to achieve as life-like a performance as possible.

Mobile Phone Announcement
All theatres nowadays will have recordings imploring people to switch off their mobile phones and anything that goes bleep. Along with television acting, mobiles are the curse of modern theatre. After a year or so on this project, we decided that

the audience were so much a part of the show, and that we were treating them so much as old friends, that one of the actors should pop out and say hello to the audience, welcome them to the theatre, and gently remind them to switch off devices that make a noise. It worked a treat. From having loads of the things squawking and ringing, we only had two or three go off in the ensuing year and a half. The most important thing was the welcoming to the theatre, of course. Making them realise they were there and we were in it together. A real person asking them politely to switch off their phone made them do so. A lesson for corporations the world over, methinks.

Notes
Most directors will watch a show or a run-through and take 'notes' on the performance and give them later to the actors or crew. Some directors write them down and give them to you, to digest in your own time; others will speak to each actor individually. Most, however, gather all the actors in one place and speak to them as a group and then give each actor notes within that context. Our Histories director Michael Boyd is not only very good at this, but particularly fond of it. I think our record was a day in rehearsals where we had a nine-hour notes session. But mornings during previews generally consisted of a two- or three-hour 'notes' session then working on stage in the afternoon – then a show in the evening.

Octology
A series of eight interconnected plays. A 'tetralogy' is four interconnected plays.

On the floor
The rehearsal room floor. The space in which to practise.

Our Man Will
William Shakespeare. House playwright for the the Royal Shakespeare Company. Pretty good at writing.

Out of Joint
Hamlet Act 1 sc 5: 'The time is out of joint. O cursed spite.'

Parley
The diplomatic 'talk' (from the French *parler*, to talk) before a battle in medieval times, to see if a resolution can be found – thereby avoiding unnecessary bloodshed.

Pavanne
An Elizabethan dance.

Phone in
If an actor turns up on stage and is sleepwalking through the lines and emotions – not properly engaging and, frankly, underselling the audience – he/she is said to be 'phoning their performance in'.

Press Nights/Days

Most shows have their 'Opening Night' after a couple of shows, or previews in the preceding few days. The Press are invited to review the show – hence Press Night – and in our case, more often than not they were invited to Trilogy Days, so our Opening Nights became more of a Day. At the RSC, there usually tends to be a week and a half of previews in order to get the thing right.

Principal

Two actors play one part: The first is the person actually playing the part on a nightly basis and advertised as such – the Principal. The second person is their Understudy.

Q & A

A question and answer session, usually held after a show, where actors and the director can face a grilling from the audience.

Rage, rage against the dying of the light

From Dylan Thomas' poem 'Do not go gentle into that good night' (1951)

Rep

Repertory Theatre. Sadly, all but died out in this country. Theatres would hire a group of actors for a season and those actors would stage a series of plays over the course of that year. Performing one play, rehearsing another and learning lines for another. Due to television, cinema and the advent of blockbuster touring shows, these theatres could not compete, so the experience of an audience following actors playing different parts over the course of a season is almost gone. Whilst it was a fantastic training ground for actors and more often than not produced high quality theatre and acting, once the theatres started having to charge serious money, people started taking notice of the sometimes variable acting this system could also produce. They could also compare it to the TV. As the reps fell out of business, one by one, so the remaining theatres and actors have had to try to up their game. The flipside of this is you still get shoddy, unlearnt, acting. However, now it's just gone on to TV and higher up the theatre chain.

Run-through

A playing of the piece in a rehearsal setting.

Seagull, The

A comedy drama by Anton Chekhov written in 1895 and first performed at the Alexandrinsky Theatre in St Petersburg in 1896. I'd never seen or read a Chekhov play, until I read *The Seagull* at college and took as read the title page which said *The Seagull: A Comedy in 4 Acts*. I thought it hilarious and wonderful in equal measure and have since been utterly perplexed by the propensity of English actors performing Chekhov to weep about the stage, wringing their hands, and whine about the lake. Lighten up, it's a comedy. We'll all get much more out of it then.

Separation

As in 'Separation, Liminality and Aggregation'. See pages 92–3.

Sonnet

A fourteen-line poem much favoured by Shakespeare who wrote, as far as we know, 154 of them.

Stalls

The area of seats in an auditorium that are level with, or sometimes just below, or nearest to, the stage. Very often the most expensive seats in the house in a proscenium arch theatre, they can also be very often the worst seats in the house in my view.

Talbot

The martial Earl of Shrewsbury who spent most of his life fighting the wars in France in the name of Henry V and Henry VI and who perished, with his son, on the battlefield. He roused the fear of God so much in the French that even to this day French mothers say the dread word, 'Talbot' to hush their children.

Tech

(Pronounced *tek*.) The abbreviation of Technical Rehearsals. In the space of three of four days (or three or four weeks if it's a big West End musical) all the technical trickery, lights and sound is plotted in and worked out by the directors, designers and actors to build the show. (See Page 28.)

Thrust

A stage which 'thrusts' into the auditorium and is therefore surrounded by the audience on three sides.

Trilogy

A series of THREE interconnected plays.

Uncut

Plays are often edited to be shorter and more concise. Uncut means they're left alone.

Understudy

Every actor may be indisposed, or 'off', at one time or another. In order for the show to carry on an Understudy will take their place. It's only really publicly funded theatre companies that can afford understudies these days – which is a big risk for all the others. And also why you sometimes see ashen-faced directors going on with the script in their hands, sweating, and desperately trying to save the show and their livelihood.

Whose mare's dead

A question asked by Falstaff in *Henry IV Part II* Act 2 sc 1 when he enters to be greeted by an argument involving Mistress Quickly and the two officers, Fang and Snare.

Yorkists

The side fighting for The Duke of York in the Wars of the Roses. They had a white rose as an emblem.